LEGATO**GUITAR**
TECHNIQUE**MASTERY**

Legato Technique Speed Mechanics, Licks & Sequences For Guitar

CHRIS**BROOKS**

FUNDAMENTAL**CHANGES**

Legato Guitar Technique Mastery

Legato Technique Speed Mechanics, Licks & Sequences For Guitar

ISBN: 978-1-78933-150-9

Published by **www.fundamental-changes.com**

Copyright © 2019 Chris Brooks

Edited by Tim Pettingale

The moral right of this author has been asserted.

www.fundamental-changes.com

Twitter: @guitar_joseph

Over 10,000 fans on Facebook: **FundamentalChangesInGuitar**

Instagram: **FundamentalChanges**

For over 350 Free Guitar Lessons with Videos Check Out

www.fundamental-changes.com

Check out the bonus videos at:

https://www.fundamental-changes.com/legato-guitar-technique-mastery-videos/

Cover Image Copyright: Shutterstock – Voyagerix

Contents

Introduction..4

Get the Audio and Video...5

Setting Up Your Tone...6

Chapter One: Biomechanics...7
Fretting Arm Positioning...7
Finger Orientation and Sound Control...9
Picking Hand Function and Control..10
String Changes and Articulation Options..11
Biomechanics Checklist...14

Chapter Two: Technique Builders...16
Chromatic Technique Drills...16
Diatonic Technique Drills..20
Sweep and Hybrid Compound Picking...25
Building A Practice Routine...27

Chapter Three: Making (and Breaking) Scale Patterns..................................29
Exploiting the Options..37

Chapter Four: Liquid Lines and Scorching Sequences...................................38
Fun with Odd Tuplets..46
Traditional Sequences Played with Legato..51

Chapter Five: Number Systems and Omissions...55
Pentatonic Number Systems...62

Chapter Six: Chromatic Passing Tones...67
Bonus Tips for Chromatic Passing Tones..73

Chapter Seven: Legarpeggios..75

Chapter Eight: Styling and Ornamentation..83
Whammy Bar Technique...83
Rubato (Robbed or Borrowed Time)..85
Burst Phrasing (Ornamentation)...87
Staccato Legato...89

Chapter Nine: Monster Licks...93
Conclusion...100
More From Chris Brooks...101

Introduction

Legato means different things to different people. According to the dictionary, legato means *bound* or *tied together*. To many musicians, it means playing *smooth* lines without a strong attack or space between notes.

To guitarists, legato is about playing those liquid lines with hammer-ons and pull-offs – the kind that recall the awe-inspiring playing of masters like Allan Holdsworth, Joe Satriani, Brett Garsed, Greg Howe and many more.

Licks are just one part of being a great legato player, however, so I wanted to create a method that delves deeply into the fretting hand mechanics, tonal control, fretboard approaches and developmental tools that can help any player create legato lines.

As you study the chapters of this book, you'll acquire a 360-degree view of playing in the legato style. The strategies contained within will most certainly have a flow-on effect in other areas of your playing, including melodic choices, musical devices, noise control and guitar tone.

Beginners can use this book to develop the essential skills required to execute legato passages. Intermediate players can advance their chops and troubleshoot existing issues they've encountered so far. Advanced players can add to their current arsenal with an array of lines from diatonic to chromatic and experiment with various fretboard strategies for new lick creation.

I hope that your study of the book will be as smooth as the licks you will create by the end of it!

Chris Brooks

Get the Audio and Video

The audio and video files for this book are available to download for free from **www.fundamental-changes.com.** The link is in the top right-hand corner. Simply select this book title from the drop-down menu and follow the instructions to get the audio.

We recommend that you download the files directly to your computer, not to your tablet, and extract them there before adding them to your media library. You can then put them on your tablet, iPod or burn them to CD. On the download page, there is a help PDF, and we also provide technical support via the contact form.

For over 350 Free Guitar Lessons with Videos Check out:

www.fundamental-changes.com

Twitter: **@guitar_joseph**

Over 10,000 fans on Facebook: **FundamentalChangesInGuitar**

Instagram: **FundamentalChanges**

Bonus videos are available at:

https://www.fundamental-changes.com/legato-guitar-technique-mastery-videos/

Or scan the QR code below with your smartphone:

Setting Up Your Tone

Before you play through the book, let's talk about pickups, pedals and amps to help you get the right tone for the right purpose.

Compression and sustain are important attributes for a legato-friendly tone on electric guitar, so it's essential to consider each component of your signal path to ensure that your sound is smooth and enables the techniques covered in the book.

Compression affects the dynamic range of a sound source, bringing dynamic peaks down in output and weaker sounds up to more regulated levels. Besides producing a more even signal saturation, compression can determine the average output of a signal. This is handy for legato playing to enable pick strokes, hammer-ons, pull-offs and slides to work in a single lick without seeming like there are stronger and weaker players on the field.

A typical signal chain for legato players includes humbucker pickups and a boost pedal running into a gain source like another pedal, or an overdriven amp. The outputs and gain settings for each component will differ depending on each player's requirements.

A bridge humbucker is very commonly used in legato for its output and tone, but a single-coil pickup with at least a moderate output and a sweet midrange EQ tone can sound great too. If you want the humbucker benefits in a single-coil space, there are lots of pickup replacement options like the Seymour Duncan *Hot Rails* and *JB Junior* as well as the DiMarzio *Fast Track* series.

From the guitar, it's important to compress the output before your signal hits the main gain stage. Running a boost pedal gives your amp a more regulated sound to amplify. Boost pedals can come in the form of *clean boosts*, which increase the output of the guitar across the board, *drive boosts* which add gain and affect tonal colour, and *compression pedals* which flatten the dynamics without changing the tone. An example of each includes the TC Electronic *Spark Boost* for a clean boost, Ibanez's famous *Tube Screamer* for drive boost and colour, and the BOSS *Compression/Sustainer* for clean compression.

When you've chosen a boost pedal, place it in between your guitar and amp but run it in bypass. Next, try setting up a drive tone on your amp. If you run a clean amp with a distortion pedal instead of a gain channel on your amp, engage it now. The amount of distortion you run at your main gain stage will depend on your genre and tastes, but the kind of tone you might use for a crunch rhythm is a good starting point.

Try some hammer-ons and pull-offs with your amp sound, then engage your front boost pedal for comparison. You should find a nice level of saturation present that enables legato without overly aggressive finger work. Tweak the drive, tone and output levels on your boost pedal until you find a tone that sounds and feels right.

If you feel that the tone is too saturated, or not saturated enough, spend a little more time getting the balance right between your boost pedal and primary gain source.

The audio for this book was recorded on a Kemper Profiling Amp using a Plexi amp sound (The 1987x profile from *The Amp Factory*) with a TS boost in front. I run the amp gain at about 60% and use the boost to add the rest of the gain and compression.

Chapter One: Biomechanics

This chapter covers the role of each hand in creating the notes for the best results in legato playing. You'll learn how to control unwanted sounds and maximise the variety of right-hand and left-hand articulation options. We'll cover,

- Fretting Arm Positioning

- Finger Orientation and Sound Control

- Picking Hand Function and Control

- String Changes and Articulation Options

By the end of the chapter, you'll understand the factors affecting your results, and be able to make some choices about how you'd like your legato approach to sound.

Fretting Arm Positioning

Optimal positioning of the fretting arm is a crucial first step in enabling your fingers to access and stretch across the fretboard. The ideal starting point involves the elbow, wrist, thumb and fingers all working together to create a good span without feeling like you need to be naturally gifted or born with big hands.

Figure 1a illustrates *ineffective* positioning. With tip of the index finger on the starting note, the rest of the index finger and the other fingers point away from higher notes along the string. The thumb is anchored gently but is resting a bit high up on the neck. Finally, the wrist is placed behind the index finger. Out of frame, the elbow usually sticks out in this position.

Figure 1a:

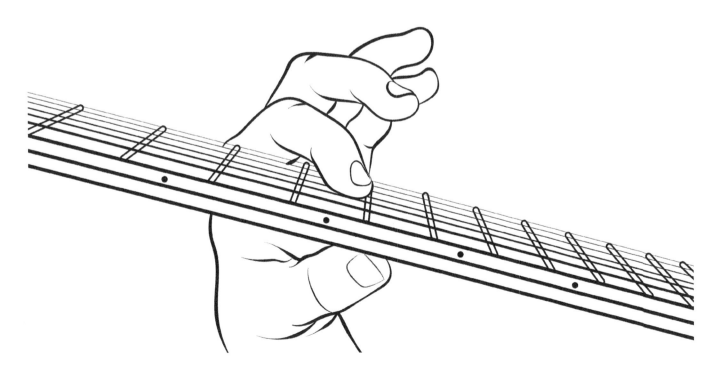

Figure 1b illustrates the result of some simple but necessary adjustments. To make these, keep using the tip of the index finger as a pivot point, but bring your elbow in towards your body. This will rotate the forearm and bring the wrist across to the other side of the planted finger. Next, place the thumb a little further up the length of the neck, and down a little on the width of it.

With the changes in effect, it should be possible to stretch from the 5th fret of the low E string to the 9th or 10th fret using the fourth finger. Even if the direction of the index finger in Figure 1a feels comfortable for the first note, you can use wrist and elbow positioning to compensate for different finger lengths as you ascend along a string.

Figure 1b:

A *hammer-on* is articulated with pressure to the fretboard instead of a pick stroke. Rather than being in place before an articulation occurs, placing the fingers on the fretboard *is* the articulation. The way you set up each finger will be crucial to producing an even-sounding hammer-on each time.

Example 1a is a basic drill you can use to test your hand position. Create a pivot point with the thumb, then use the elbow and wrist to roll each finger onto the fretboard, one at a time. A standard error is to lock the wrist into a rigid position and expect finger strength to produce all the motion. On the 8th fret pull-off back to the 5th fret on both strings, avoid any drastic dragging motion that would cause you to play out of tune or with too much pressure.

Example 1a:

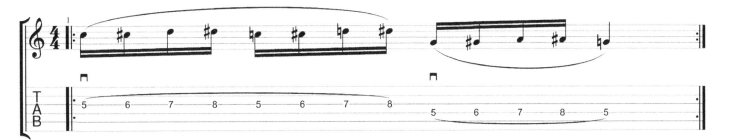

Finger Orientation and Sound Control

With the softer dynamics produced in legato playing, it's vital to preserve an acceptable signal-to-noise ratio i.e., maintaining the integrity of the notes compared to ringing strings or other noise issues.

We will explore the interplay between the left and right hands for noise control shortly, but for the fretting hand, let's look at how positioning and the combination of fingertips and pads help maintain the purity of legato notes.

Figure 1c illustrates two examples of finger orientation. On the left, a note on the D string is fretted using only the tip of the index finger. Fretting this way opens up the possibility of accidental noise from the pick, the other fingers, or even just the vibration of the instrument.

On the right-hand side of Figure 1c, the same note is fretted using a blend of the tip and pad of the index finger, controlling the strings beneath with a soft muted barre. No pressure need be applied to the other strings. A fingertip/pad blend can be incorporated into fretting with the other fingers too, but the index finger often does the lion's share of this noise control.

Figure 1c:

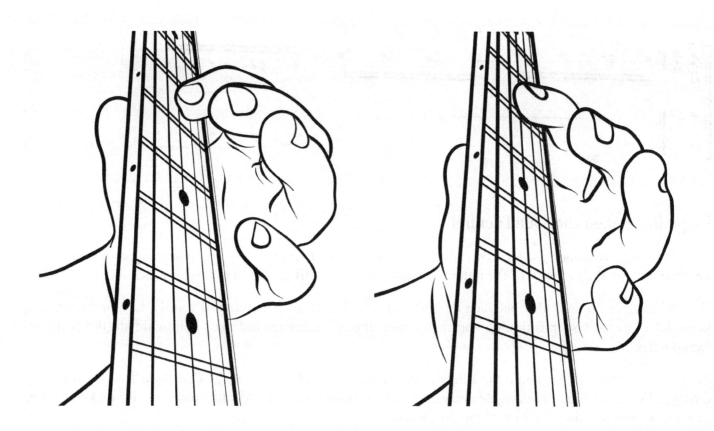

String-muting devices are commonly seen wrapped around guitar necks these days. Replacing the humble sock that many studio and home recording guitarists have used over the decades, elastic hair bands and commercially available Velcro wraps are often placed around the first fret of the fingerboard to deaden open strings or unwanted string noise.

Many people frown upon string-muting devices, they can be either a crutch or a useful tool depending on how much they are relied upon.

Picking Hand Function and Control

While the picking hand doesn't articulate each note in legato playing, it does play a big part in control, dynamic variation and trading off with the fretting hand to mute unused strings.

Picking hand functions used in this book can be divided into the following tasks:

- *Plectrum Initiation*: Many players use pick strokes at the beginning of strings to create the initial vibration that slurs will follow

- *Hybrid Picking:* Some players, especially in the Fusion genre, incorporate fingers of the picking hand into note articulation for a different attack

- *Palm Muting String Control:* When fretting higher strings, palm muting unused lower strings is a crucial noise deterrent. As licks descend to the lower strings, a balancing act occurs as the mute rolls off the strings to allow the fretting hand clean access to the lower register. The fretting hand then takes care of unused higher strings in noise control

- *Staccato Legato:* The term is an oxymoron, but in Chapter Eight we'll be using the picking hand for some muted legato to create a more extensive dynamic range within hammer-ons and pull-offs.

Example 1b will help you test the changing roles in sound control between the picking hand and the fretting hand. As you begin at the high E string, use your picking hand to mute everything from the B string to the low E string. When it's time to play the B string on the 3rd beat of bar one, roll the palm mute away from the B string and let the index finger of the fretting hand gently mute the high E string beneath.

As you descend to each new string, progressively roll away the palm mute so that by the time you play on the low E string, only the fretting hand controls the notes played, and the strings muted beneath. Avoid using barre-chord levels of pressure on the strings not being played. A light amount of contact on any otherwise noisy strings is all that is necessary.

Example 1b:

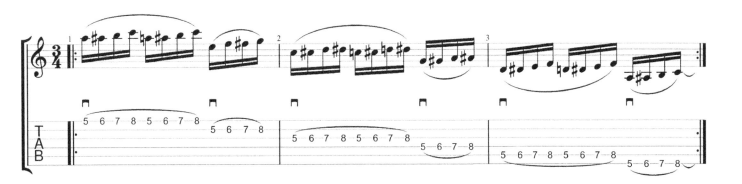

String Changes and Articulation Options

Before getting into the technique drills in Chapter Two, it's necessary to consider some options that not only require slight variations of technique but have flow-on effects on your personal tone, style and how you approach the chapters ahead.

To explore and discuss, here's a drill that will be repeated using various articulation techniques.

Example 1c:

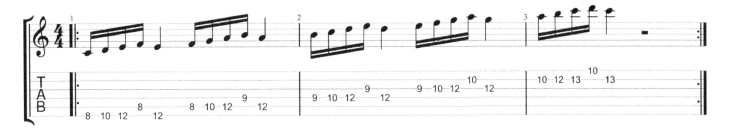

Articulation option 1 uses pick strokes to initiate the first note of each string, with hammer-ons used along each string where applicable.

Example 1d:

It's becoming more common in the fusion world to use picking hand fingers to replace upstrokes, so option 2 uses a finger to initiate the higher string of each pair, indicated with a *P* which you can think of as a *pluck*.

While the second finger is the closest available finger to the pick, I prefer the third finger for adjacent strings because of its similar length to the index finger. When you see the P indicator, use your preferred finger for picking.

Example 1e:

Because the fourth finger of the fretting hand has plenty of leverage, it is often unnecessary to initiate vibration on a lower string with a pick stroke. Option 3 in Example 1f uses a *hammer-on from nowhere* for each 1/4 note in the phrase. From now on, try to initiate lower strings this way unless otherwise indicated or impractical.

Example 1f:

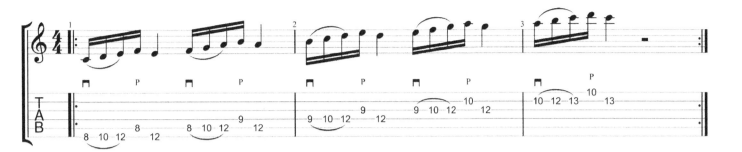

Option 4 is to use hammer-ons from nowhere for strings in either direction. A purely hammered approach requires each finger to apply enough pressure to produce notes, but not so much that each note sounds *slammed* down on the fretboard.

A legato effect should be maintained with string changes. Remember that legato means tied together, so the notes should meet up without space between them or any ugly-sounding overlap.

Example 1g:

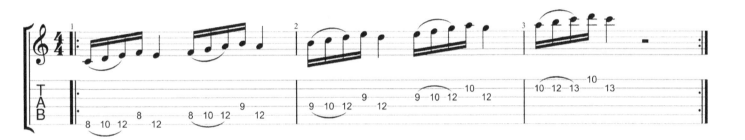

Using all hammers is excellent for strength building and also to become mindful of how little attack is required from the pick or fingers in the legato sound.

Descending Hammers

The hammer-ons from nowhere approach has applications in descending along strings too. *Re-hammering*, as it's sometimes called, is adopted by some legato players instead of overt pull-offs to replicate the evenness of Jazz horn playing and to create a consistent tone in any direction.

To apply descending hammer-ons, hammer each new note at the precise moment the finger on the previous note is lifted (not pulled). With a little development time, you might conclude that pull-offs don't need to be extreme in your playing to be effective.

Listen to the audio of Example 1h, which is performed with the same tone: firstly with pull-offs on the descents, and secondly with hammer-ons only.

Example 1h:

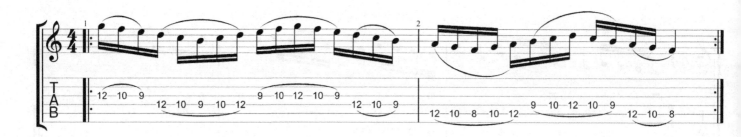

The late, great Allan Holdsworth, a pioneer of this approach, reportedly detested the sound of fingers pulled off the string to generate notes. By contrast, '80s high gain rock and shred guitar players often use pronounced pull-off sounds in descending lines. In the middle, some players who are credited as hammer-only exponents perhaps just use a light touch and less-obvious pull-offs.

My own view? It's important not to gate-keep a technique. It belongs to all of us. There are degrees of touch available, and it's essential to use what sounds and feels right to you. With so many great legato players out there, from jazz-inspired to extreme rock, it's part of your journey to either emulate or revolt against what those before you have done.

For future examples in the book, remember that you have the option to:

- Use pick strokes on each new string

- Use pick and finger strokes on each new string

- Begin lower strings with hammer-ons from nowhere

- Begin any string with hammer-ons from nowhere

- Use re-hammering to replace pull-offs

Experimentation is highly encouraged with each and all of the approaches!

Biomechanics Checklist

Before moving into the development drills that will fill your initial practice routines, check that you have accomplished the goals listed below as they will put you in good stead for the material in Chapter Two.

Goals:

- Establish functional and practical fretting using finger, wrist and elbow placement

- Master your fretting angles using the right balance of fingertips and pads to control adjacent strings

- Build a tag-team between fretting hand control and picking hand muting

- Begin strings using pick strokes, finger plucking and hammer-ons from nowhere

- Know the difference between pulling off and rehammering notes

Keep in mind:

- Once you know all the options, techniques become choices rather than laws

- Your preferences will help build your style and sound

Troubleshooting

- *Bad tone*: experiment with the interaction between your boost pedal and amplifier. Reconsider the gain, tone and volume settings in your setup and ensure that even a single note sounds pleasant.

- *Messy execution*: roll the gain back and spend more time on the Chapter One examples, taking care to fret each note cleanly, with the picking hand muting unused strings. Bring the gain back up and monitor the signal to noise ratio in your playing.

- *Legato timing*: try using the pick for each note, removing it on selected repeats until you can play the legato version exclusively with the same command of timing.

Chapter Two: Technique Builders

The exercises in this chapter focus on building technique for both hands using the principles covered in Chapter One. Through a variety of chromatic and diatonic drills, you will be able to construct your first legato practice routines that will develop hammer-ons, pull-offs, hammer-ons from nowhere, legato slides and hybrid picking.

To keep the examples clean for reading and open to personalisation, the tablature purposely avoids the clutter of excessive pick stroke indicators and other playing directions unless they are the specific target of development.

In cases where I've indicated my personal preferences, try the suggestions offered, then adopt any changes you wish to make as your chops develop and lead you in your own direction.

Chromatic Technique Drills

The first three examples draw from chromatic patterns in 7th position with a 1-2-3-4 finger allocation. Try each drill using a downstroke and a hammer-on, keeping pick strokes soft and moving from string to string smoothly with a sweep-like motion. For bonus practice, repeat the drills using both hybrid picking and hammer-ons from nowhere to begin each string.

As the drills move from the low E string to the high E string, mute each lower string with the picking hand when it's no longer in use.

Example 2a:

Example 2b is a variation which uses the third and fourth fingers on the lower string of each pair. If the discrepancy between the lengths of the third and fourth digits is a hindrance, remember to use your wrist to level the playing field.

Example 2b:

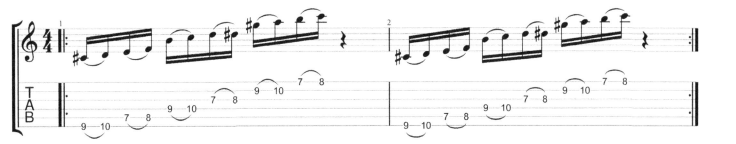

Dividing the fingers into different pairs, Example 2c begins with the first and fourth fingers, then the second and third fingers. Bar two switches the pairs.

Example 2c:

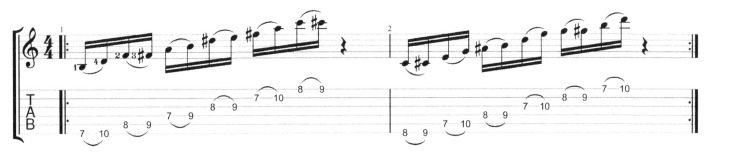

A *pull-off* requires a slightly different approach to a hammer-on because you will need to place the *catching note* (i.e., the note you will hear after the pull-off) right before you pull the higher finger away from the string.

In a descending chromatic exercise like Example 2d, you might be accustomed to stacking all four fingers on the fretboard and peeling them off one by one. Instead, use only the fingers required to play the pair of 1/8th notes in each beat. Doing so allows more flexibility in the wrist and less tension throughout several repeats.

Example 2d:

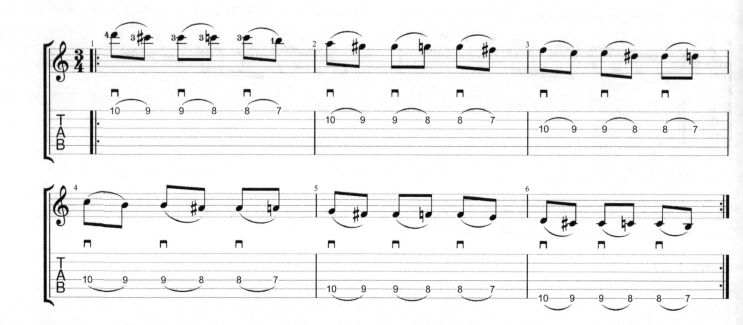

Example 2e combines the rolling hammer-on and pull-off approaches within chromatic stacks along each string. Long streams of slurred notes can be trickier to play in uninterrupted time, so try not to float around rhythmically.

Example 2e

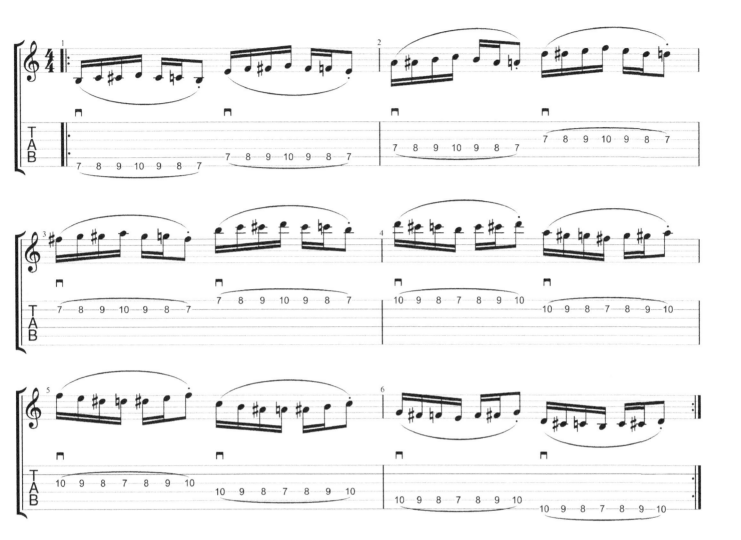

Example 2f is one of twenty-four chromatic fingering permutations and works well as a drill for pull-offs or exclusive hammer-ons. On the audio, you will hear a light pick stroke on the first note of the high E string, followed by soft pull-offs and hammer-ons with each new string initiated using a fourth-finger hammer-on from nowhere.

Example 2f:

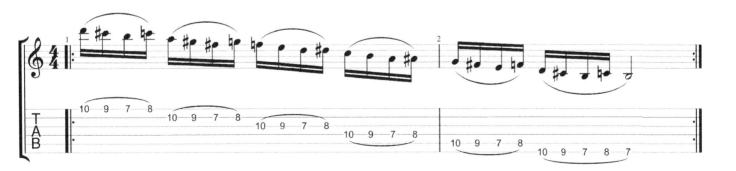

For extra chromatic homework, try replacing the previous example with some or all of the following twenty-four permutations. From 1-2-3-4 to 4-3-2-1 they are:

1-2-3-4	1-2-4-3	1-3-2-4	1-3-4-2	1-4-2-3	1-4-3-2
2-1-3-4	2-1-4-3	2-3-1-4	2-3-4-1	2-4-1-3	2-4-3-1
3-1-2-4	3-1-4-2	3-2-1-4	3-2-4-1	3-4-1-2	3-4-2-1
4-1-2-3	4-1-3-2	4-2-1-3	4-2-3-1	4-3-1-2	4-3-2-1

Before moving on to diatonic legato drills, let's use the fretboard simplicity of chromatic ideas to focus on some hybrid picking with Example 2g.

Bars one, two and three allow time to prepare the alternating pick and finger strokes that occur on each 1/4 beat. In bars four, five and six, the fingerpick stroke at the beginning of each two-beat phrase is immediately followed by a downstroke of the pick. This half of the drill may require more focus to achieve speed, so isolate the latter portion of the drill for further development if necessary.

Example 2g:

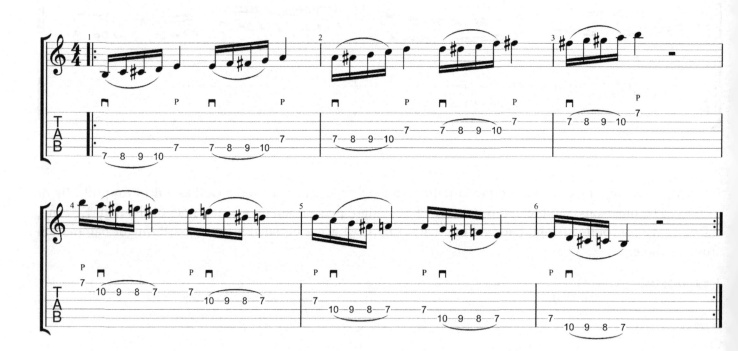

Diatonic Technique Drills

It's time to apply legato building to small licks that fit into everyday keys and expand them into complete scale lines. The exercises in this section will build stamina and improve string-changing.

These examples will draw on various three-note-per-string shapes within the key of C Major and its modes.

C Major Scale Across The Fretboard

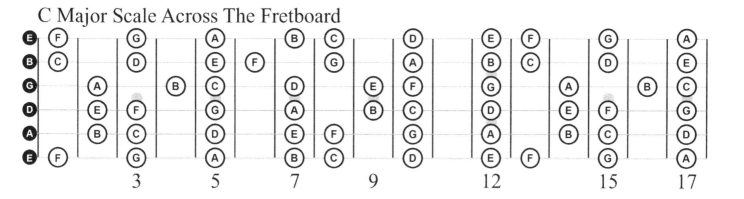

Example 2h will develop into a six-string sequence throughout the next few examples but begins as a two-string drill using two whole-tone stretches on both the D and G strings. These are fretted with the first, second and fourth fingers.

Example 2h:

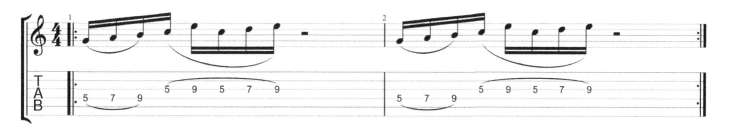

Expanding the lick to loop back to the starting note, both strings include two extra notes. Use a fourth finger hammer-on from nowhere to re-engage the D string on the third 1/16th note of beat 4 in both bars.

Example 2i:

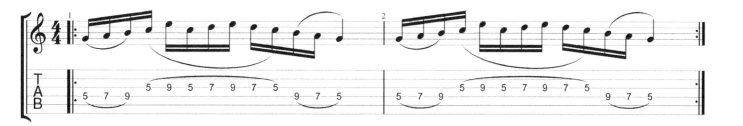

In Example 2j, returning to the 5th fret of the D string in bar one, beat 4 begins a repeat of the lick. The pattern crosses the bar line into the second measure, concluding on the 9th fret of the G string on beat 4.

Example 2j:

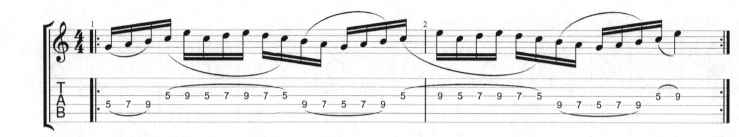

Moving through three octaves, Example 2k uses a similar motif to Example 2g, beginning on the G notes located on the 3rd fret of the low E string, the 5th fret of the D string and the 8th fret of the B string. The index finger will begin each octave of the lick.

Example 2k:

Diatonically transposing the previous lick upward by one pattern in the key gives us a shape consisting of a whole tone and semitone spacing on each string. Some players may prefer to use the first three fingers to fret this pattern but, in practise, use it as an opportunity to strengthen the changes between your third and fourth digits using the fingering suggested.

Example 2l:

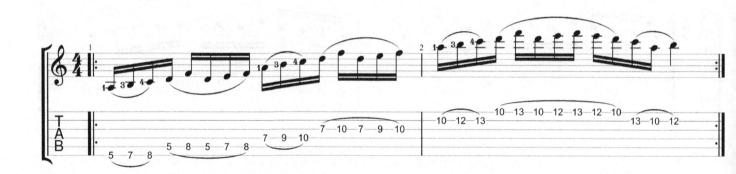

Let's use one string pair to try all the different combinations of two-fret and one-fret spacings that occur in diatonic three-note-per-string shapes.

Example 2m:

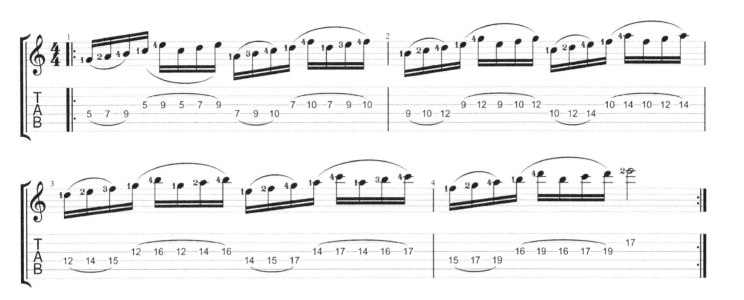

Legato Slides offer a way to connect patterns and avoid getting stuck using the same numbers of notes per string. Since you won't be picking your way through position shifts, it's essential to keep enough pressure on the fingerboard as you slide.

Example 2n includes a legato slide on the D string from the 10th fret to the 9th fret in both bars.

Example 2n:

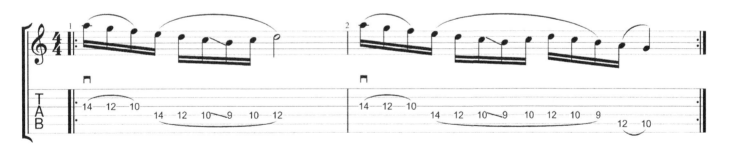

Taking legato slides through six strings, Example 2o uses an eleven-note pattern that repeats in a lower octaves and string pairs each time. Aside from the first note, each string change is initiated with hammer-ons from nowhere.

The notation in this example uses the odd time signature of 11/16 to help you isolate each octave for separate practice. In more practical usage, players like Richie Kotzen and Steve Vai might rush the phrase to force the eleven 1/16th notes into two beats of a 4/4 bar, as in Example 2p.

Example 2o:

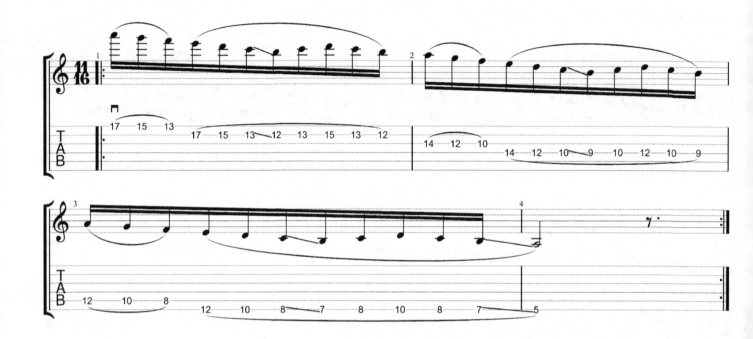

Example 2p:

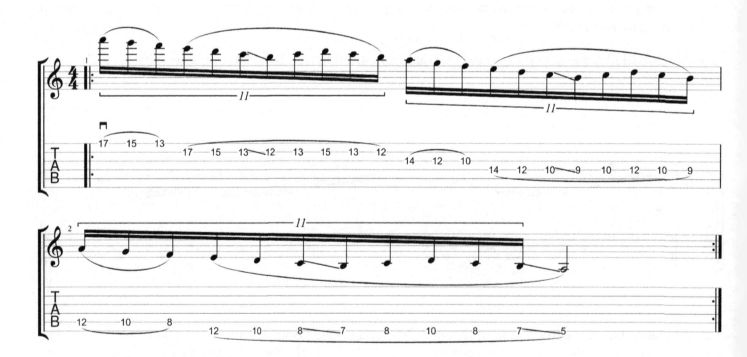

Let's try ascending slides in Example 2q. With four notes each on the low E and A strings, this C Major pattern moves from the 8th position to the 12th position. Often, but not always, the highest finger used along a string will slide up in an ascending position shift, and the lowest finger will slide down in a descending shift. For lone notes like the 12th fret of the G string in bar one, I generally use a finger pluck.

Example 2q:

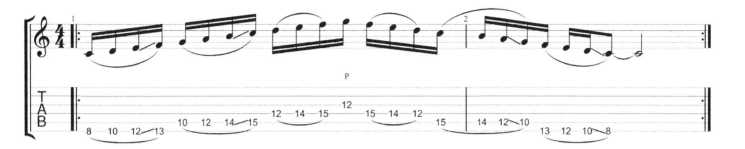

Using four notes on every string, the A Minor pattern in Example 2r starts in the 5th position but finishes up in the 17th position. Try sliding with the fourth finger as indicated but, as an alternative, compare it to sliding with the index finger between the first two notes of each string.

Example 2r:

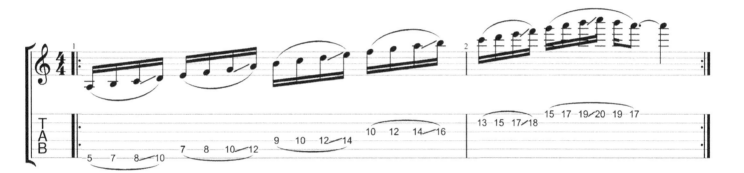

Sweep and Hybrid Compound Picking

A variant of hybrid picking switches between sweep picking and fingerpicking. The internet uses the term *Swybrid* picking to describe this compound of directional pick strokes and finger strokes. For legato playing, it can be useful to have a few moves like these to expand string-changing options.

Example 2s begins each eight-note unit with two downstrokes. Each note on the G string is played with a pluck of either the second or third fingers of the picking hand while the return to the D string starts with a hammer-on from nowhere.

For the sweeps, keep in mind that directional pick strokes should see the pick land on each new string as soon as it leaves the previous string. Avoid separated pick strokes.

Example 2s:

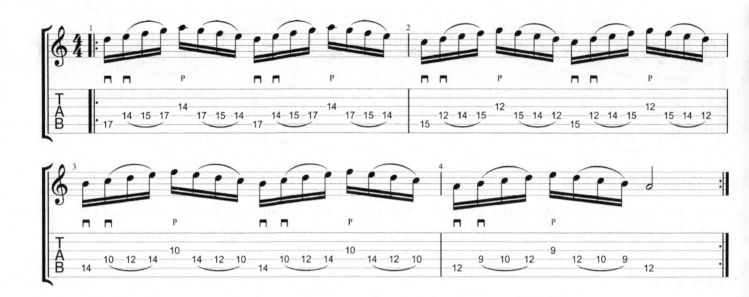

Example 2t ascends using a downstroke through the low E string and A string, a second-finger stroke (*m* or *medio*) on the D string and a third-finger (*a* or *annular*) stroke on the G string. This 50/50 split between pick and fingers creates tonal contrast and makes it simple to put the pick in position for each repeat.

All downward string changes are handled with hammer-ons. The notation here is in 7/8 time to make it clear where the pattern repeats. The fourteen-note phrase can be played in 4/4 time too, which will see it crossing the bar line at a different point with each repeat.

Example 2t:

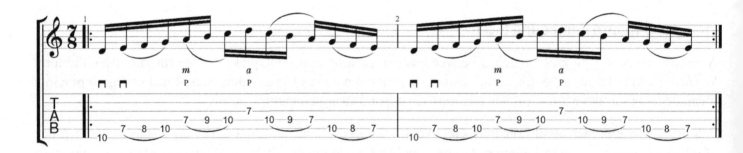

Upward sweeps can be incorporated into Swybrid string changes too. In Example 2u, the ascent from the A string to the D string uses the pick, second finger and third finger with an upward sweep from the D string to the A string, then to the low E string after two pull-offs.

Example 2u:

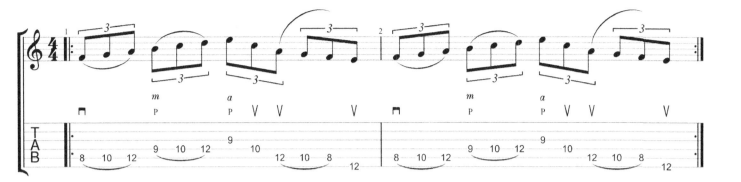

Building A Practice Routine

Practice sessions are often compared to training sessions at the gym. I use this analogy as well, not because guitar requires strength training, but because a good practice session requires structure to enable progress.

As you acquire more material to practise on guitar, life often dictates that your available time does not increase at the same rate. It's important to cycle exercises through your allotted practice time, replacing redundant material with new challenges.

I believe a good practice routine consists of something familiar, something unfinished, and something brand new. Not every session needs to stick to a formula, but a ratio approach might help you decide what should be tackled and what should be left behind. Applying these three attributes in a practical way might look something like this:

• Familiar: Use exercises you know well to warm up for the day's work

• Unfinished: Improve material you've begun already in previous sessions by developing it further, playing it faster, moving it to other keys etc.

• New: Prepare yourself for the next challenge by starting something brand new as a preview of future practice sessions

At the beginning of your legato development, all of the material in this chapter might be brand new, but even after a few days of practice, drills that used to fall into the *new* category can now be used as warm-ups. When an exercise becomes easy, it's time to replace it with another.

There are seven chromatic drills in this chapter. If each was assigned one minute of practice time, that's a seven-minute warmup. From there, you might spend ten minutes looking at the first five diatonic technique drills. Finally, a three-minute peek at the next few diatonic drills caps off a twenty-minute legato practice session.

Next week, you might be finished with the chromatic drills and, instead, promote the diatonic exercises to warmup-material status, using the bulk of practice time to work on the scales in Chapter Three. Cycling material helps your progress without the need for more time.

Be your own personal trainer when it comes to practice. Decide when a portion of the program has served its purpose and move ahead with new challenges. Remember that growth occurs outside the comfort zone.

Exercises in this book should be learned in free time to get the mechanics right before bringing out the metronome. If you find *click, click, click* uninspiring to practice to, check out the unaccompanied drum tracks in the audio of this book.

In the next chapter, you will learn to unlock the fretboard in major and minor keys using (and then losing) common and unorthodox scale patterns.

Chapter Three: Making (and Breaking) Scale Patterns

This chapter will help you put in place systems to navigate the fretboard in a thorough way to avoid limiting yourself to specific patterns or positions.

Good command of fretboard mapping allows you to make choices about where you play the notes you wish to use. Using Example 3a to illustrate this point, here are six pathways for a two-octave C Major scale. Each pattern has a slightly different timbre, layout, application of pick strokes and string changes.

Example 3a:

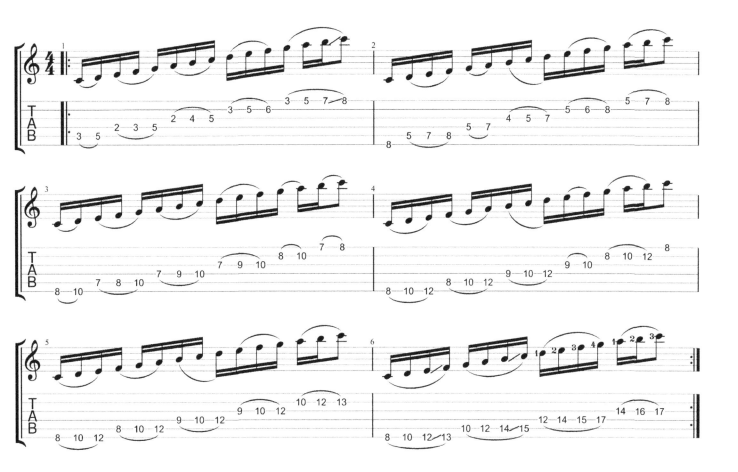

By the end of this chapter, you should be able to make choices about scale playing from various fretboard options. You can achieve this by mapping out the key of C Major in the common three-note-per-string (3NPS) patterns, then exploring the impact of using two- and four-note-per-string patterns.

Covering the key of C Major from the root note position, the seven 3NPS patterns look like this:

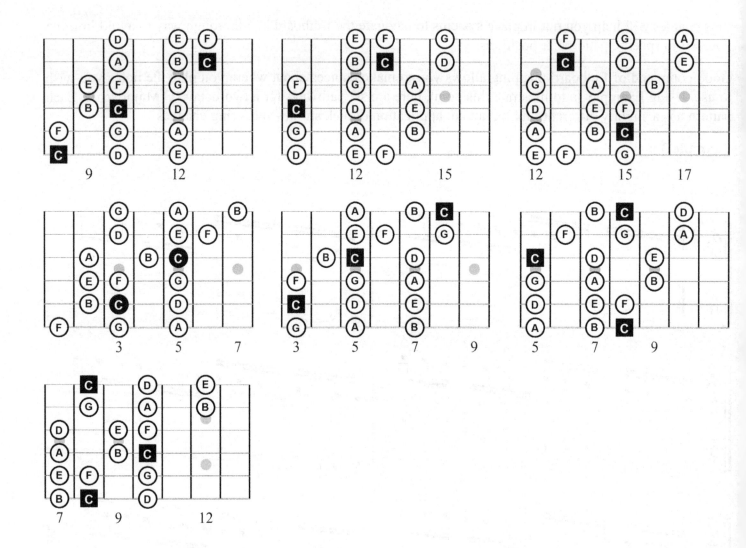

The numbering consistency and possibilities for applying sequences make the 3NPS system a favourite among rock players. Musically, each pattern contains two full octaves plus an extra four notes. To make sure you can connect each pattern to the next, take a look at Example 3b which begins on the fourth pattern.

This drill ascends and descends in alternating fashion by connecting each pattern with a legato slide. Ascending string changes use the pick while descending string changes begin with a fourth finger hammer from nowhere. Notated with 3/4 time signature to confine each pattern to a bar, you can play these patterns in any time signature as long as you maintain an even rhythm between each hammer-on, pull-off and slide.

Example 3b:

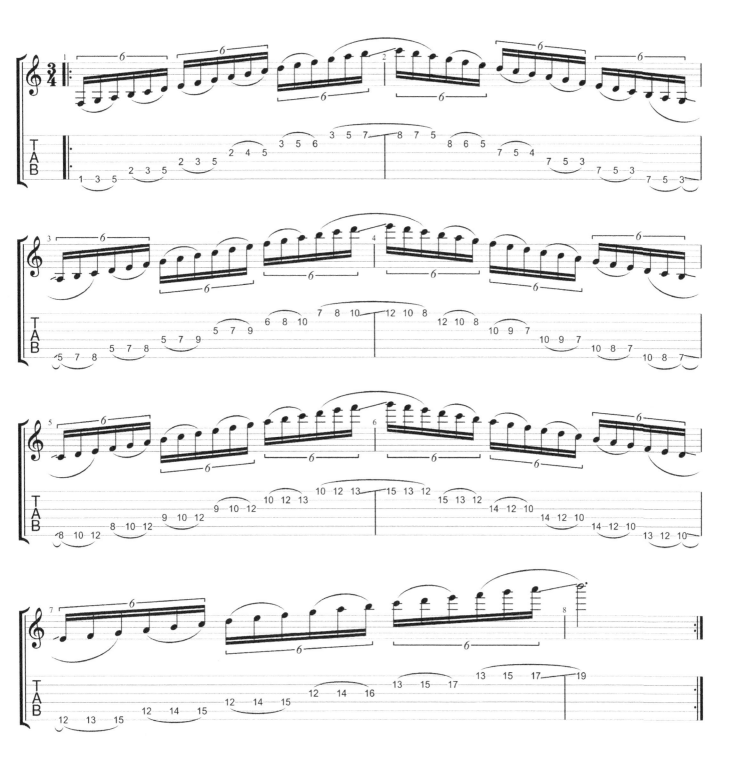

In the previous example, it was the fourth note on the high E string of each ascending pattern that created a position shift. We can use this trick to jump patterns at any point within a line.

Example 3c includes four notes on the A string, G string and high E string to enable us to move between four of the previous 3NPS patterns.

Example 3c:

Example 3d applies the same concept in both directions, using index finger slides on the B string, D string and low E string and fourth-finger slides on the A string, G string and high E string.

Example 3d:

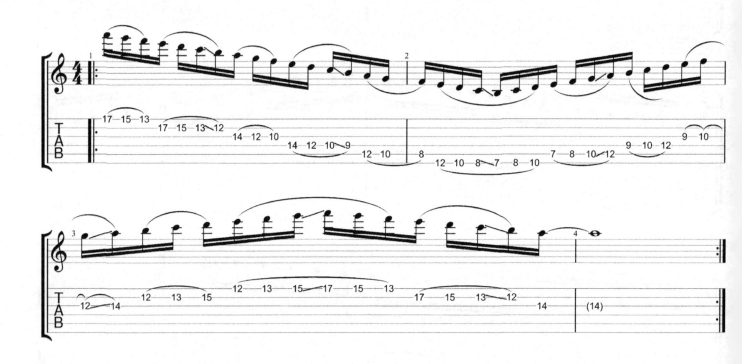

Changing positions and directions at various points, Example 3e is a great lick for creating a rollercoaster feel as you ascend and descend within an overarching upward direction. As you piece together longer and faster lines like this, you should begin to feel more fretboard freedom and flow between patterns.

Example 3e:

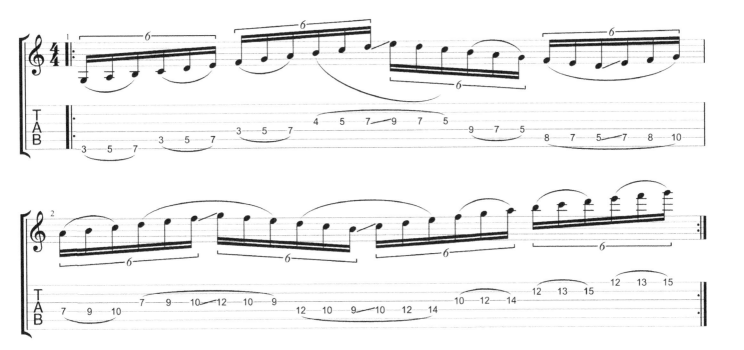

Playing four notes on a string needn't always include slides. While some patterns require quite a stretch to place four fingers along one string, a less strenuous example can be found from the 2nd and 6th degrees of a major scale (the notes D and A in the key of C Major). From both degrees, notes can be fretted a whole tone up, a semi-tone above that, and another whole tone higher, allowing the notes to roll on and off with the fretting hand.

In Example 3f, use your fretting hand wrist to roll each new note onto the fretboard, releasing the previous note so that you don't have to stretch across five frets on the low E string, D string and B string. Using the wrist will also make it easier to swiftly position your index finger onto the other strings, which require a smaller span.

Example 3f:

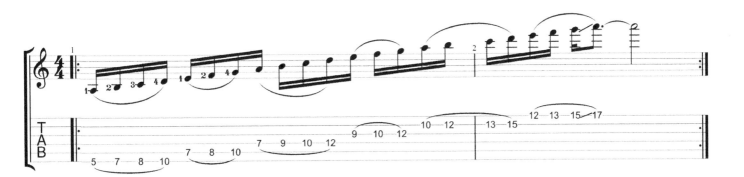

Let's try rolling back and forth within the larger stretch in Example 3g. Beginning with the D note on the 10th fret of the low E string, be sure to keep the fretting hand relaxed by lifting off each finger that is no longer needed. When fretting the three notes on the higher string of each pair, use fingers one, two and three for continuity with the other strings.

Example 3g:

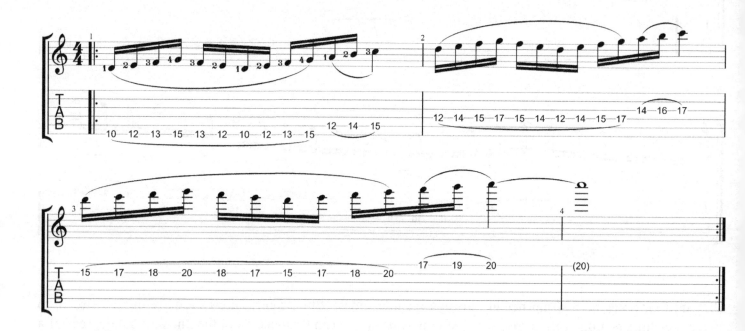

While scales played with 3NPS stay relatively in position and scales played with 4NPS shift upward or downward in the same direction as the last note on the string, two notes per string (2NPS) have yet another effect on fretboard positioning.

Ascending 2NPS diatonic scales will begin each new string in a lower position than the previous string in almost all cases. Descending scales have the reverse effect. Playing exclusively in 2NPS is not a common approach for major and minor scales but is worth exploring as an escape route from other pattern forms.

Example 3h is a routine ascent and descent using 3NPS, beginning on the F note on the 13th fret of the low E string, peaking at the C note on the 17th fret of the G string. We can compare this to a 2NPS approach in the next example.

Example 3h:

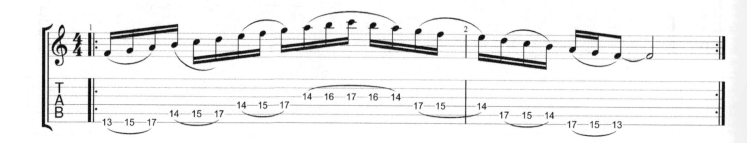

Containing the same notes, Example 3i is by no means a fast alternative but creates a different timbre as the scale cuts across all six strings in the ascent, two notes at a time. Upon leaving the high E string, we can connect to the descending 3NPS pattern that begins in bar one, beat 4 on the second 16th note.

Example 3i:

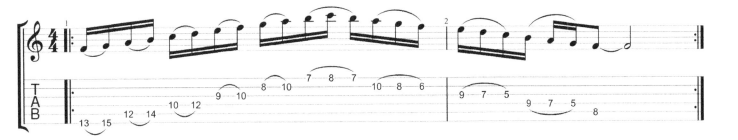

Combining the 2NPS approach with alternating three- and four-string groups, Example 3k again begins on the 13th fret of the low E string, concluding on the 1st fret an octave lower. Rather than view this example as an exercise in speed, use it to expand your scope of how notes connect on the fretboard.

Example 3j:

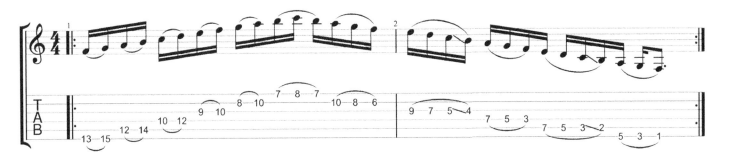

In Example 3k, an ascending 3NPS pattern beginning in 3rd position is escaped in bar two using descending two-note units on the high E string, B string and G string. The D note on the 7th fret of the G string is also the first note of a four-finger pattern up to the 12th fret, enabling another position shift for the remaining strings.

Example 3k:

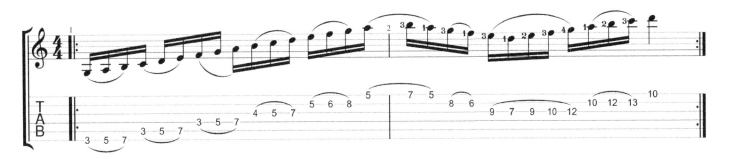

Two notes on a string occur systematically in the CAGED system as the 5th and 6th degrees of the scale occupy their own string in each pattern. If you've memorised the seven 3NPS patterns, it's easy to see how CAGED patterns that share the same starting notes will shift down into different 3NPS patterns any time a two-note string occurs.

In C Major, the five CAGED patterns are:

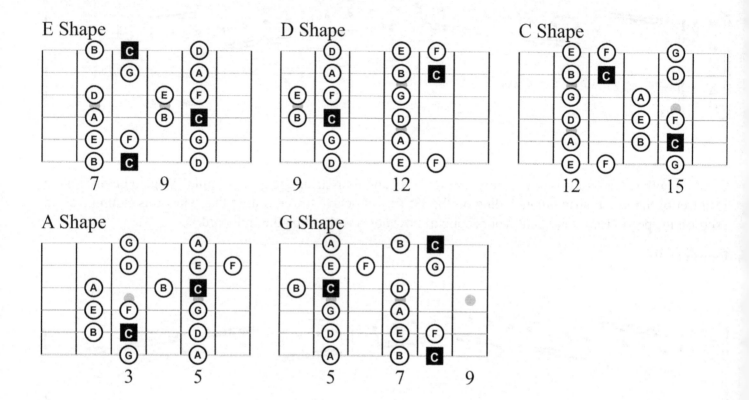

To summarise the theme of making and breaking patterns, Example 31 includes various numbers of notes per string and positions, executed with hammer-ons, pull-offs, slides and four-finger fretting.

On the strings containing four melody notes, pay attention to the presence or absence of position slides as the latter will be your cue to use a 1-2-3-4 fingering over the whole tone/semi-tone/whole tone stretches using the wrist-rolling approach.

Example 31:

Exploiting the Options

The critical takeaway in this chapter is that versatility and flexibility will help you transcend the limitations of *systems* and keep you mindful of the endgame: complete fretboard mastery. You can achieve this in manageable steps by learning patterns, then learning not to be limited by them.

Using the shapes in this chapter and also the fretboard map at the beginning of Chapter Two, aim to complete the following list, slowly at first, moving to a moderate tempo.

• Play the seven 3NPS patterns in the key of C Major, ascending and descending

• Play the five CAGED patterns, ascending and descending

• Use four notes per string to any time escape other patterns

• Use two notes per string momentarily to shift downward on the fretboard when ascending, or upward on the fretboard when descending

When you've completed the above list, move on to Chapter Four to build a library of sequences and develop some serious speed!

Chapter Four: Liquid Lines and Scorching Sequences

With your technique developed and fretboard knowledge expanded, it's time to arm your lead playing with a selection of slick legato licks and sequences applicable to soloing.

Sequencing is a way of breaking up streams of consecutive scale tones by running different intervals or motifs through steps within the scale. By restating a theme or melodic passage in rising or falling steps, we can combine unity of concept with variety of pitch.

It's crucial to experiment with and document your own legato sequences to build a library of ideas, but I'm going to start you off with many of my own in this chapter. You'll also learn my legato approach to common sequences that are generally approached with picking.

Each sequence example is applied to a scale pattern within the key of C Major, but you are encouraged to apply each concept to every scale and mode in your repertoire. A suggested chord is included for practice, but you should try each example over various chords in the key and develop your own preferences.

My four-step approach to coming up with new sequences is:

1. Create a *unit*: a motif that will be moved up or down within the scale

2. Apply the unit to positional scale patterns

3. Extend the range of the sequence by cutting across scale patterns with the unit

4. Try the complete sequence in different subdivisions, e.g., 1/16th notes, 1/8th note triplets, 1/16th note triplets etc.

In Example 4a, the ascending C Major Pattern 1 is broken up with a twelve-note unit in string pairs. Taking place over 2 beats, each repetition of the unit goes up to the fourth note in each string pair, down to the first note, then back up to the sixth note. In the tab and audio, single notes on higher strings are finger-picked.

Example 4a:

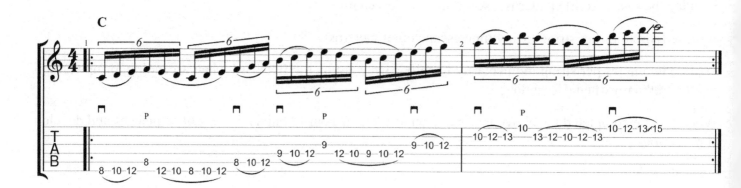

To cover more fretboard territory with the same sequence, Example 4b cuts across patterns to create a three-octave hexatonic pattern (using six diatonic notes out of seven in each octave), ending on the 20th fret of the high E string rather than the 15th.

Example 4b:

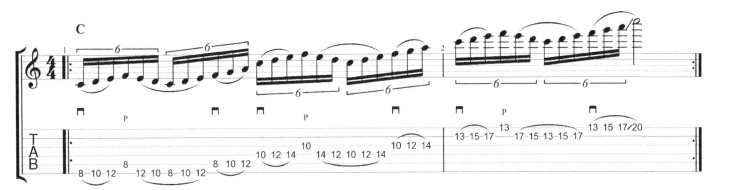

It's a good idea to have sequences that run in the opposite direction to your favourites. Reversing the note order of the core unit of the sequence is an excellent place to start.

Example 4c is a descending run designed to connect to Example 4a. When played after the previous example, a slide into the first note of this lick will get things moving. If adhering to the suggested sweep picking strokes, use a soft pick attack.

Example 4c:

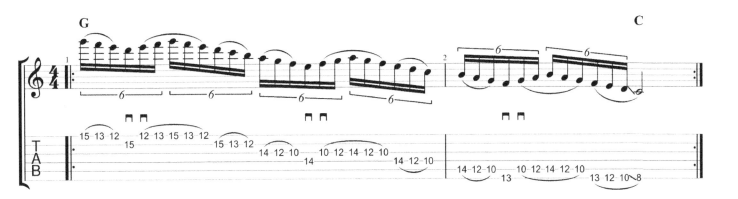

Using the sixth 3NPS pattern of C Major, Example 4d is played in 1/16th note triplets like the last three examples but uses a nine-note unit that is applied to five-string pairs. The result is a sequence that sounds displaced because each unit takes place over one and a half beats – a less predictable way to sequence.

Example 4d:

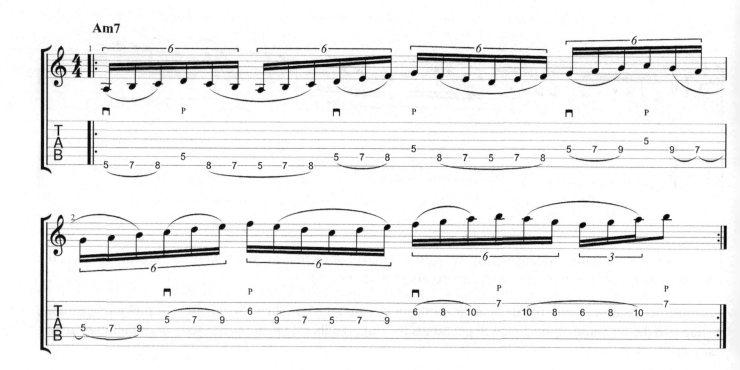

As a descending counterpart to the previous sequence, Example 4e reverses the nine-note unit and applies it to the fifth 3NPS pattern. Because single notes appear on lower strings in this direction, a two-string sweep is used to keep the momentum of the sequence. Keep picking attack discreet to maintain smoothness.

Example 4e:

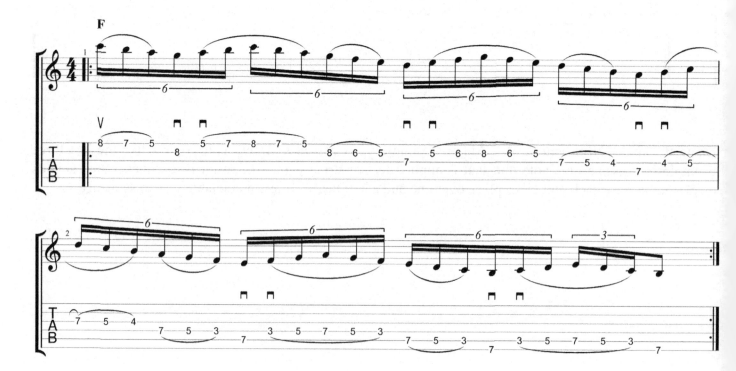

As the string layout in Example 4f indicates, the next sequence uses a melodic unit of six in another hexatonic pattern. While it works well as a sextuplet-based lick, the goal here is to maintain rhythmic control independent of the melodic unit. To avoid slipping into six notes per beat, tap one foot in 1/4 note beats, developing a feel for which notes fall on the beat.

Example 4f:

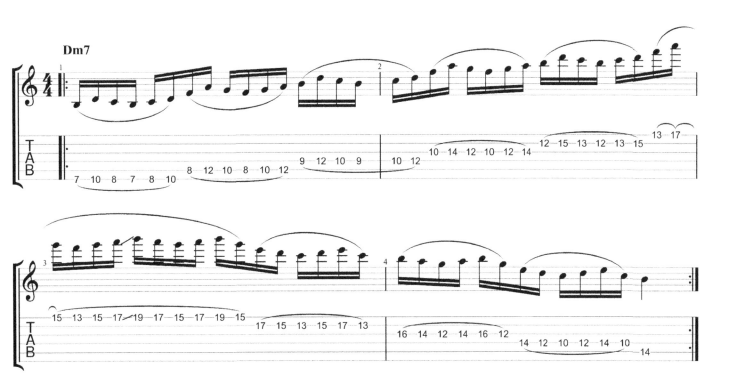

Instead of using the displacement sound of the previous examples all the way through, a *reset* can be used to begin sequences on downbeats again. In bar one of Example 4g, the nine-note motif is cut short on beat 4, with only six notes used. A position shift to the 7th fret of the D string in bar two begins a new iteration of the phrase, an octave higher than bar one.

Mechanically, each nine-note unit uses one downstroke, one finger stroke, and one hammer-on from nowhere.

Example 4g:

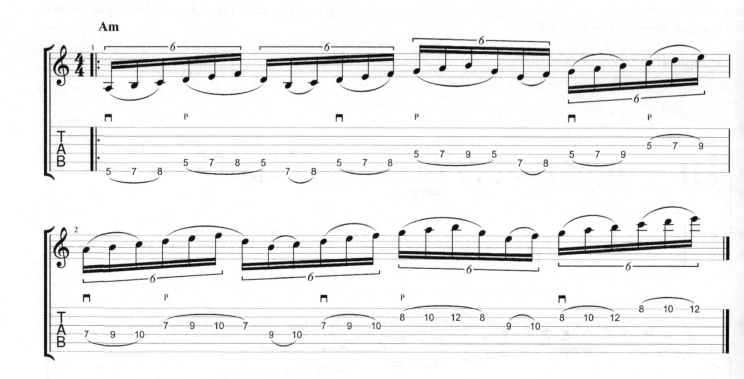

As a companion sequence to connect with Example 4g, Example 4h also uses two nine-note units followed by a group of six notes before a pattern switch in bar two.

As a descending line, there's lots of leverage to hammer on from nowhere when engaging lower strings. The notation and the audio for this example outline my own approach, which applies to both bars.

Look out for the fingerpicking on the first note of beat 1, the third note of beat 2 and the sixth note of beat 4. The pick strokes used in beats 2 and 4 could just as easily be replaced with hammer-ons from nowhere, but a downstroke right after a finger-picked note has a nice contrast.

Try a few mechanical approaches (including all hammers) and see what resonates with you.

Example 4h:

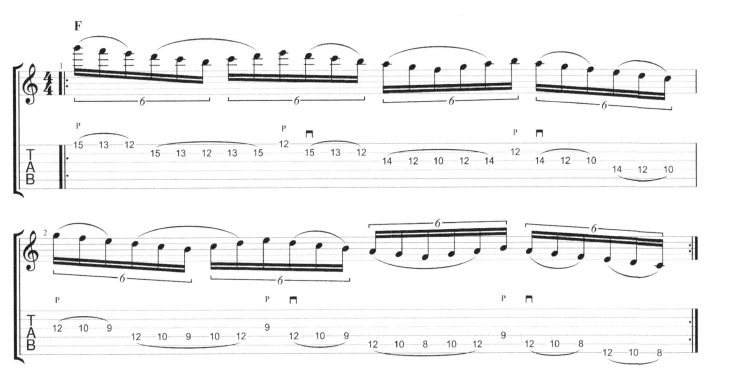

If you've been shying away from the hybrid picking suggestions so far, Example 4i might sell you on the approach. Using the third finger of the picking hand to pluck the single notes that pop up on the higher string in each bar uses less movement than pick strokes only, allowing faster and efficient string changes. Experiment with dynamics and see if you can reduce the volume of the hybrid picking to that of the slurred notes.

Each unit in this sequence begins a 5th higher than the previous step. In several cases, you will be rolling the fourth fretting hand finger across adjacent strings, so be careful not to overlap the notes. In bar four, a B note on the 7th fret of the high E string helps avoid an awkward reach to the 12th fret of the B string.

Example 4i:

Getting back to 1/16th note subdivisions, Example 4j features an eight-note, two-string unit that *could* be used in a positional scale pattern. Instead, this lick takes the unit a diatonic 6th higher each time until the end of bar two, then shifts down the B string and high E string in diatonic thirds through bars three and four.

Example 4j:

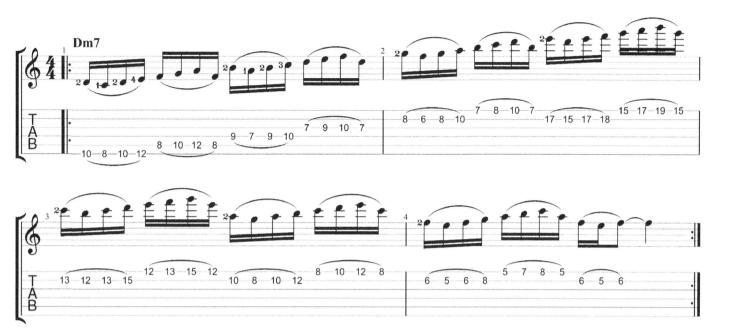

Using a 4NPS pattern with an eight-note sequential unit, Example 4k is a good test of fretting hand stamina as you work from the 19th fret of the high E string to the 3rd fret of the low E string. By now, you should find this possible without pick strokes, except for the first note in bar one.

Example 4k:

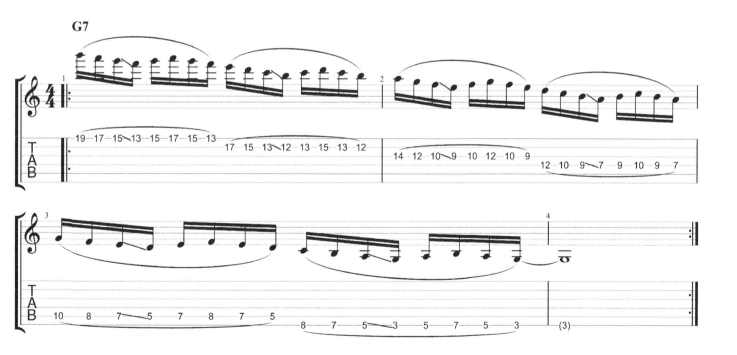

1/16th note sequences that change with the beat can sound a little too much like exercises after a while. A simple way to freshen things up is to displace the notes before or after a downbeat. Example 4l does this with the previous sequence, starting on the -*and* of the 1st beat in bar one.

Example 4l:

Fun with Odd Tuplets

For sequences based on melodic units of numbers like five, seven and nine, a rhythmic approach popular among legato players is to play the odd groups of notes within beats using tuplets or *artificial divisions*. Rather than have the melodic units *spill over* the beats, artificial divisions will see numbers like five, seven, nine or eleven notes take place within the space that four or eight notes might otherwise occupy.

Example 4m shows what a five-note melodic unit looks like when played as 1/16th notes.

Example 4m:

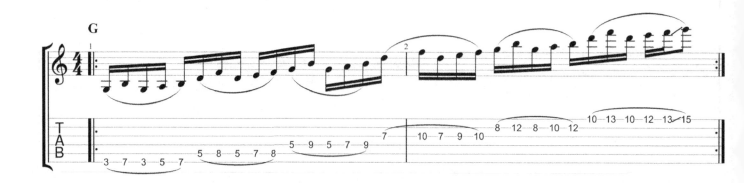

Fitting each five-note group into single beats (Example 4n) creates a rhythmic ratio of 5:4 called *quintuplets*, giving the previous sequence an accelerated feel that ends more than one beat sooner. The result is a more exhilarating sound.

Example 4n

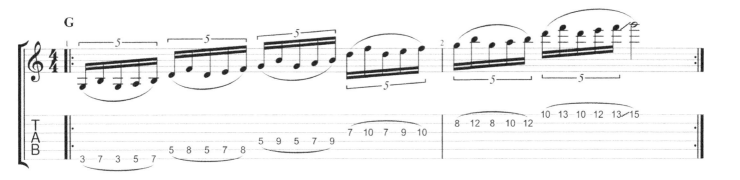

Your logical mind might attempt to break quintuplets into a pair of 1/16th notes and a set of 1/16th note triplets, but such an approach sounds quite different to five evenly placed notes. To help develop a more even distribution of quintuplets, play Example 4n again slowly, tapping your foot on each string change, which coincides with each beat. You can also try speaking any five-syllable phrase repeatedly and evenly. A made-up phrase of mine goes *Si Ki Ta Ka Ta*.

Try descending in quintuplets using the two-string unit in Example 4o. This time, string changes and beats are not mutually exclusive.

Example 4o:

Septuplets are another artificial division, comprised of seven 1/16th notes over a 1/4 beat. Example 4q runs a septuplet motif through the sixth major scale pattern and incorporates Swybrid technique into the execution.

To prepare for the full sequence, Example 4p isolates a portion for development. Take note of the three articulation points using the pick and one finger. The pick stroke on the last note of beats 1 and 3 sweeps through to begin beats 2 and 4. In the longer version (Example 4q), each sweep will initiate another septuplet.

Example 4p:

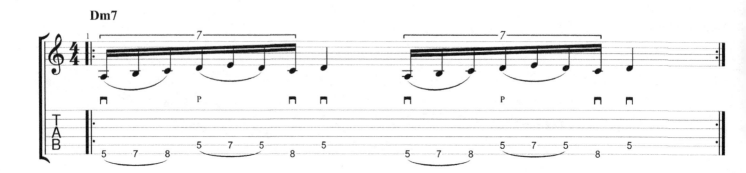

Example 4q:

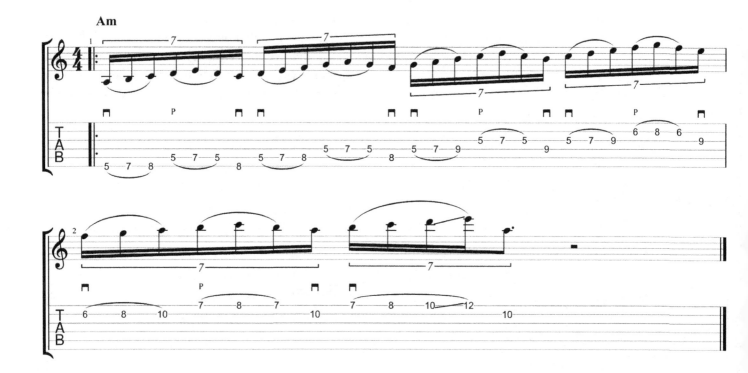

Flipping the motif to create a descending counterpart, Example 4r can mostly be played without pick strokes, but I prefer to outline the groups of seven in the manner indicated.

Example 4r:

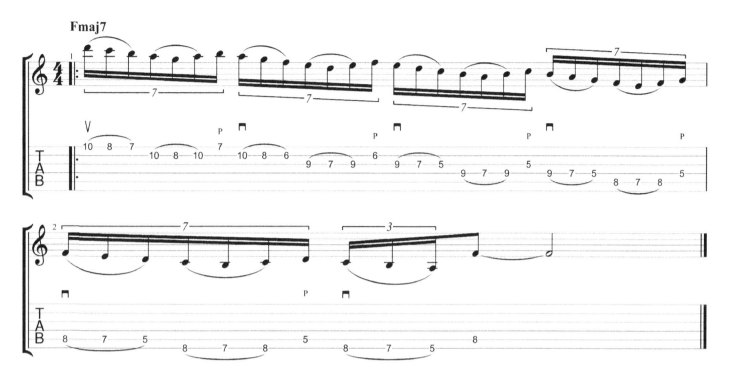

Nonuplets or nine-note tuplets are interesting because unlike quintuplets and septuplets, they are divisible by the common rhythmic number three. Depending on the subdivisions, nonuplets can be thought of as three lots of three or a *triplet of triplets* spread over two beats or one beat.

1/16th note nonuplets take place over two 1/4 note beats. The first, fourth and seventh notes in each nine also coincide with 1/4 note triplets. Consider the following:

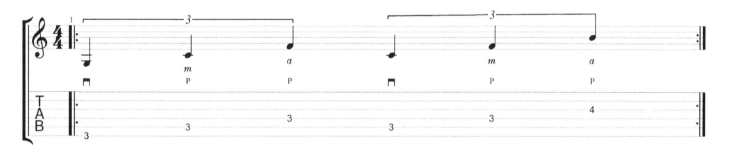

Using the 1/4 note triplets as marker points, try Example 4s. You can reinforce the *three x three* approach by using the pick, 2nd finger and 3rd finger to pick each of the marker points, followed by two hammer-ons for each string. The beams in the notation also serve as a visual reference for this approach.

Example 4s:

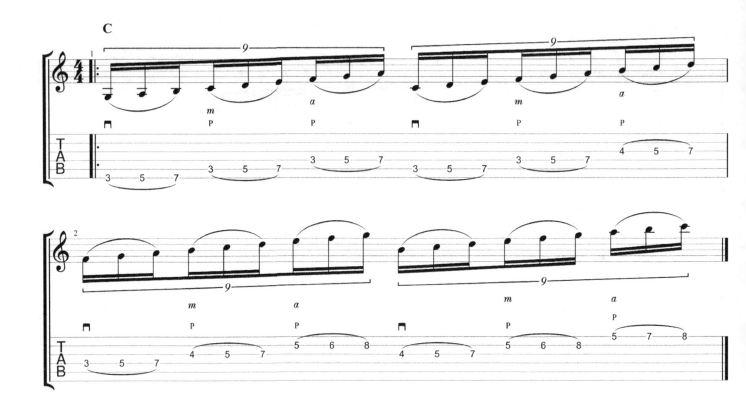

Although tempo will place limits on the use of 1/32nd note nonuplets, the *triplet of triplets* approach works using 1/8th note triplets as the basis for the nine 1/32nd notes that will occur in each beat. Each of the notes in the following bar becomes a marker point for the nonuplets in Example 4t.

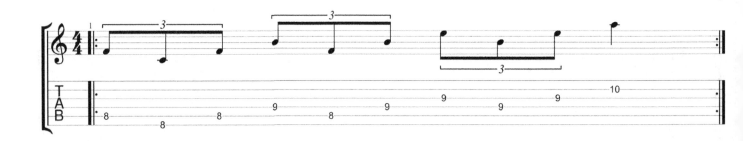

Example 4t:

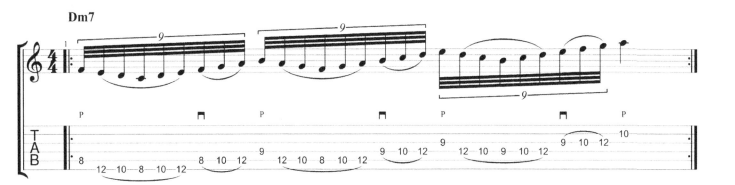

Traditional Sequences Played with Legato

Sequences that are often used as picking exercises or phrases can also be adapted to a legato approach with the tools you've developed in this book.

Ascending and Descending Fours

Using each note in the scale to launch four ascending notes in each step is commonly executed with alternate picking. In Example 4u, a sweep/hybrid picking approach is taken, with each mechanical template taking place over three beats. The example is written in 3/4 time to make the mechanical repeats obvious.

Example 4u:

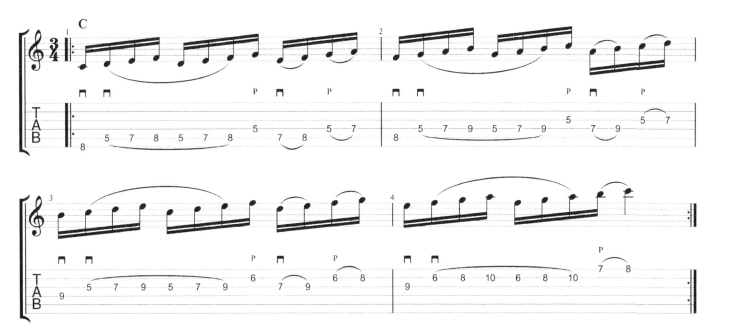

The descending fours pattern in Example 4v also uses Swybrid execution and fits perfectly with Example 4u for combined practice.

Example 4v:

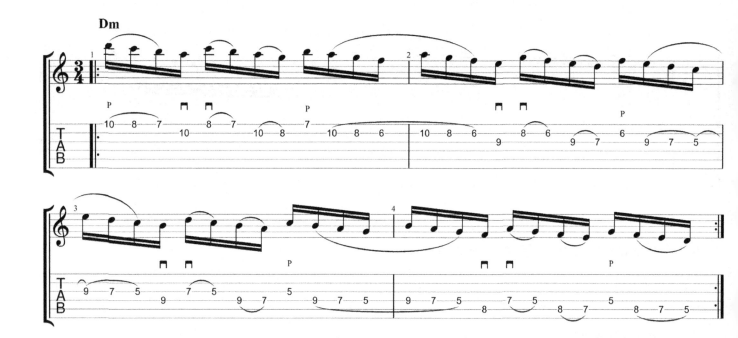

Ascending and Descending Threes

For moving up and down the scale in threes, sweeping also comes in handy for string changes.

In both the ascending (Example 4w) and descending (Example 4x) versions, the G string is used as a position-changing point between the fifth and sixth patterns of the C Major scale. Instead of slides, the position shifts are handled with the fingering changes indicated.

Example 4w:

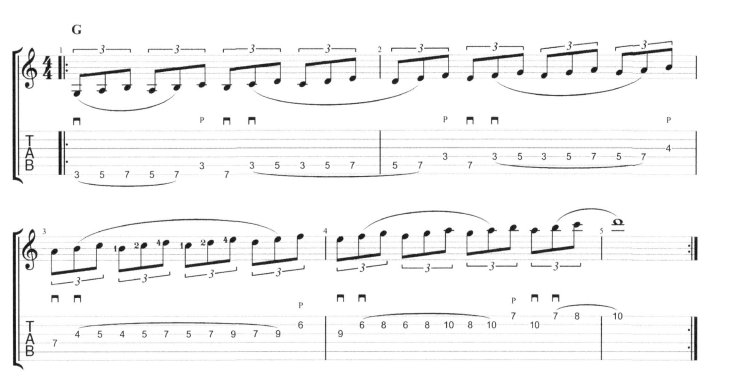

Example 4x:

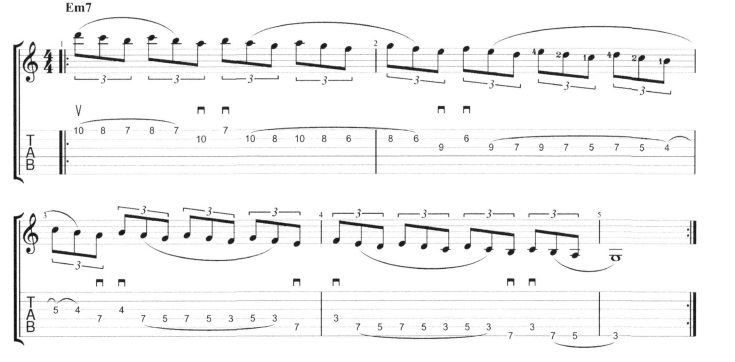

Ascending and Descending Seconds

Based on an intervallic approach, the last example of this chapter moves descending diatonic 2nds up the scale in bars one and two, then ascending seconds going down the scale in bars three and four. Swybrid picking is used in the ascent, but only sweep picking strokes are required in the descent.

Example 4y:

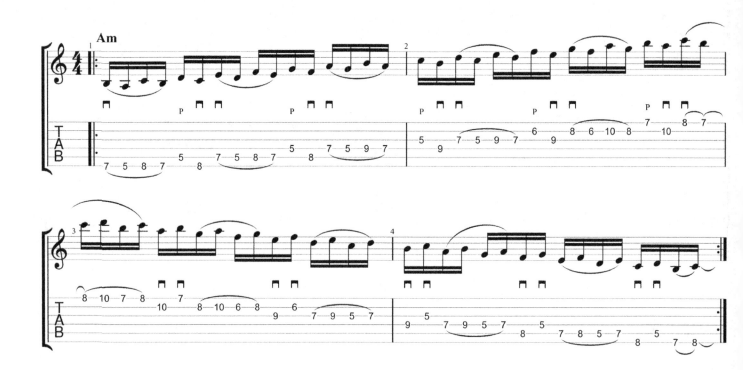

To make the most of the sequences in this chapter, apply your favourites to each scale you regularly use. Draw on whole and partial sequences in improvisation and aim to connect them fluently with the other concepts used in your solos.

Next, create and catalogue your own sequences, incorporating different intervals, tuplets and scale shapes to build a vocabulary that is uniquely your own.

Chapter Five: Number Systems and Omissions

In the previous section, you learned to break out of up and down scales by applying motifs, sequences, melodic displacement and odd tuplets. This chapter looks at another way to avoid playing consecutive scale notes by systemising mixed numbers of notes per string.

Using numbers to decide what notes you play sounds decidedly unmusical and very much a *guitar player thing* to do. What number systems *can* do, however, is force us to look beyond our established playing habits and explore options which might then form musical choices. By omitting notes with these systems, something as simple as playing up and down sounds more appealing. When sequencing, even more melodic interest is created.

In each system, the numbers are listed from the low E string to the high E string. In the examples, expect to see some overlap between different scale patterns to produce practical and musical results. When you can play the examples, experiment with substitute note choices if you find other preferences within the number systems presented.

System One: 1-3-1-3-1-3

Alternating between one and three notes per string is a handy way to move within a position in fewer steps than an entire scale but preserve a linear sound more scalar than an arpeggio lick.

Starting from a D note on the 10th fret of the low E string, Example 5a ascends using a sweeping downstroke for string changes and can use an upward sweep or hammer-ons from nowhere for descending string changes. This lick sounds excellent over a IIm chord because the notes used belong to a *minor eleventh* arpeggio. The pattern in this example draws from the first and seventh C Major scale shapes.

Example 5a:

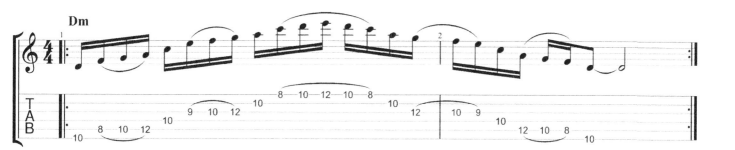

Let's apply a five-note motif to each of the three-note strings in the ascent. Example 5b takes a little longer to get to the highest note in the lick but creates musical interest and variation from the normal descent.

Example 5b:

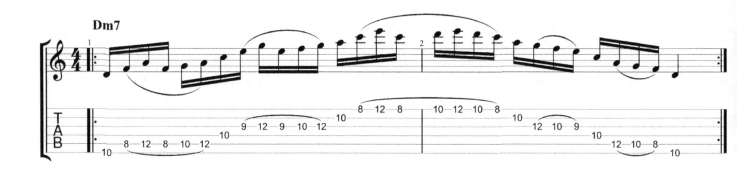

Next, let's sequence in both directions. In Example 5c, an ascending motif weaves through the first fourteen notes of bar one, beginning a new iteration on the third 1/16th note of beat 4. In bars three and four, the descending fourteen-note unit travels from the high E string to the D string, then from the G string to the low E string.

Example 5c:

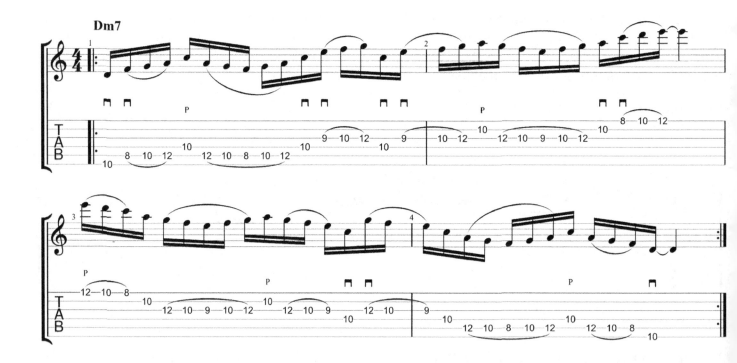

System Two: 3-1-3-1-3-1

Flipping the order of where the numbers occur, System Two outlines slightly different notes in each string pair. Using the II chord again for comparison, Example 5d starts with three notes on the low E string, one note on the A string and follows in alternating fashion across the other strings.

Example 5d:

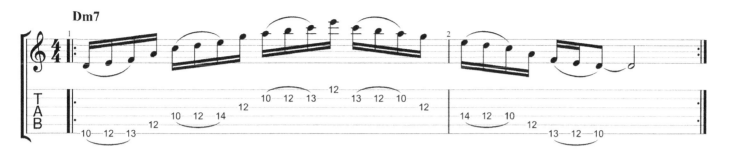

Sequencing your way through a mix of consecutive scale notes and diatonic 3rds with the 3-1-3-1-3-1 format creates licks that can sound more complicated than they actually are. With a combination of one, three and five notes per string at various points, Example 5e demonstrates the benefits of using a number system layout while still sounding creative.

Example 5e:

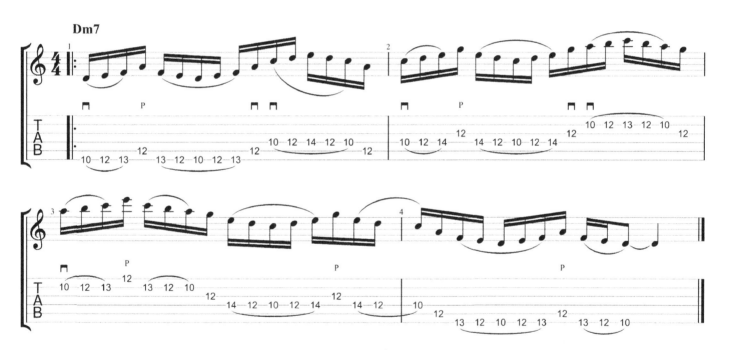

Transposing the format to suit a dominant chord, Example 5f works nicely over a G7 chord while drawing on notes from the fourth and fifth 3NPS patterns of the C Major scale.

Example 5f:

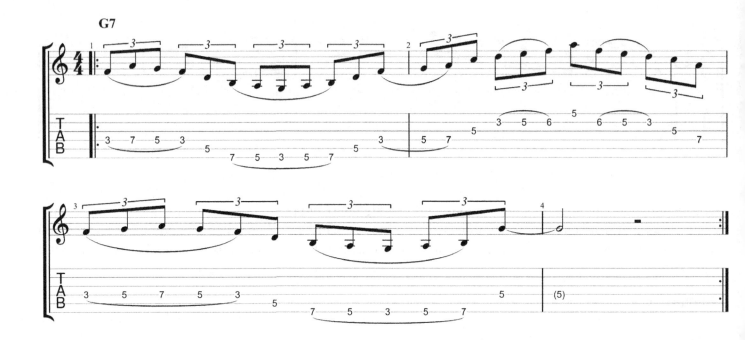

Thinking in combinations of *three* and *one* can work in horizontal position shifts and still sound perfect over a single chord. Using three melody notes each on the A string and G string and one note each on the D string and B string, Example 5g traverses three positions that begin on triad tones of the F chord underneath (F, A and C).

Example 5g:

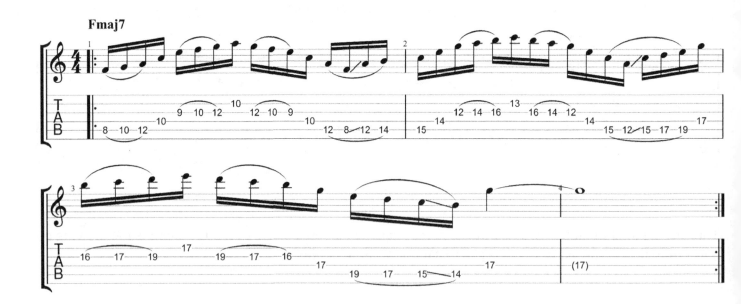

System Three: 3-1-3-3-1-3

The third system draws from both of the previous formats by having 3-1-3 on the bass strings and 3-1-3 on the treble strings. Selecting notes from the 8th position using this form, Example 5h ascends and descends while Example 5i applies a more creative approach.

Example 5h:

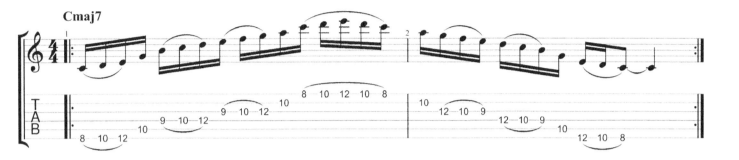

Example 5i:

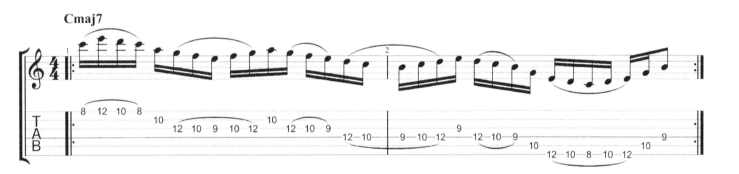

Example 5j breaks positions by using the 3-1-3 format from the low E string, then the A string, the D string and finally the G string. Each time, the seven-note melodic unit is diagonally transposed a 5th higher. The lick concludes on the 19th fret of the high E string, giving the lick a twelve-fret span.

Example 5j:

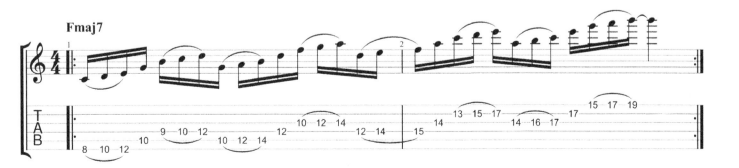

Example 5k applies descending 3-1-3 forms to the sixth, seventh and first 3NPS patterns of C Major.

Example 5k:

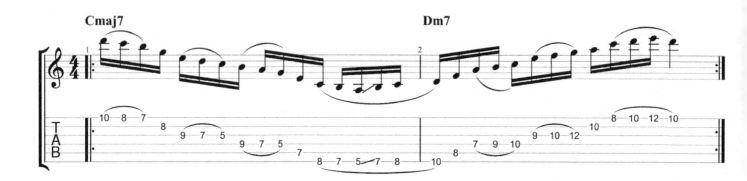

System Four: 4-1-4-1-4-1

I use this system to move five notes through three-octave patterns. In the four-note groups, slides can be placed at the beginning or end of each string.

Example 5l:

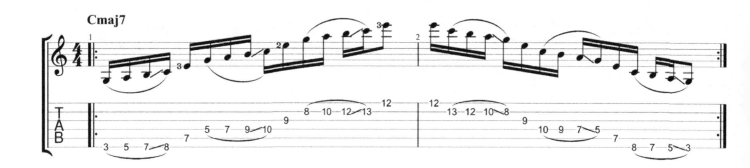

A longer ascending path can be created with a few detours on the way up, with Example 5m taking two bars to reach the highest note in the pattern.

Example 5m:

Example 5n transposes the 4-1-4-1-4-1 concept a diatonic 3rd higher than the ascending pattern in Example 5l, placing the slides at the semitone intervals this time. Example 5o represents a more lick-oriented descending version.

Example 5n:

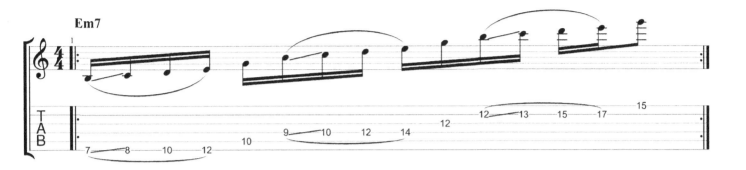

Example 5o:

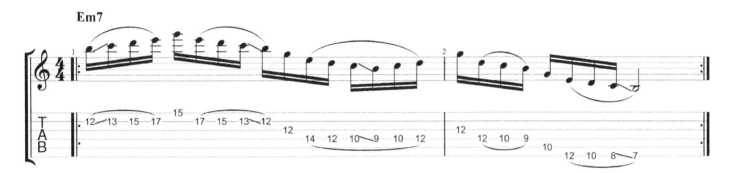

Sequencing along each four-note string, Example 5p re-introduces 1/16th note nonuplets rhythms, each taking place over two beats.

Example 5p:

Pentatonic Number Systems

Number systems make the Pentatonic scale a powerful tool for legato playing. Because pentatonic scales only contain five notes, number systems can be used to play the full scale across all strings without any omissions.

Example 5q demonstrates how the 3-1-3-1-3-1 format can cover the same notes as the standard A Minor pentatonic box. The key of C Major contains the notes of two other pentatonic scales (D Minor and E Minor pentatonic), so if the stretch in this example is too wide for now, transpose it a perfect 4th or perfect 5th higher.

Example 5q:

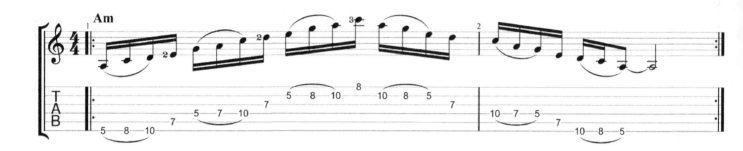

Using the E Minor pentatonic scale in the 12th position, Example 5r shows a very different side to the pentatonic than the blues-based runs commonly played within the *box shapes*.

Example 5r:

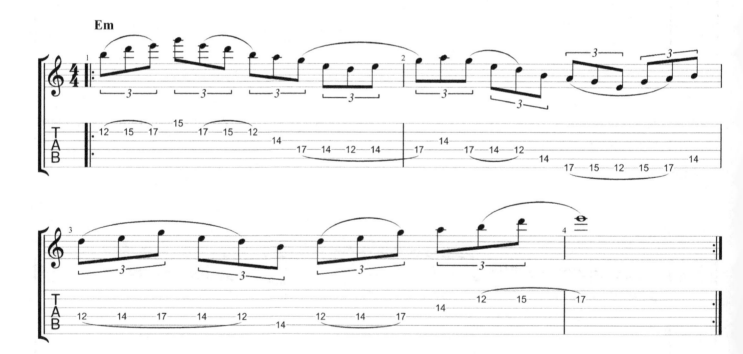

Beginning with the D Minor pentatonic in 10th position, Example 5s brings Swybrid chops to the pentatonic realm with a repeating motif in bar one. The next bar shifts to E Minor pentatonic to copy the previous phrase before ascending to the high E string by beat 3.

Example 5s:

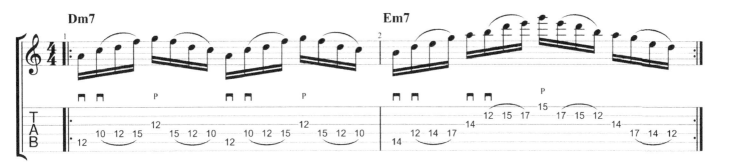

Where 3-1-3-1-3-1 pentatonic forms kept the pattern within one position, 3-1-3-3-1-3 pentatonic patterns break out by connecting to a higher pattern on the treble strings to reach two extra scale notes.

Compare Example 5t with the shape used in Example 5q. When you've memorised the differences, proceed with the sequence in Example 5u.

Example 5t:

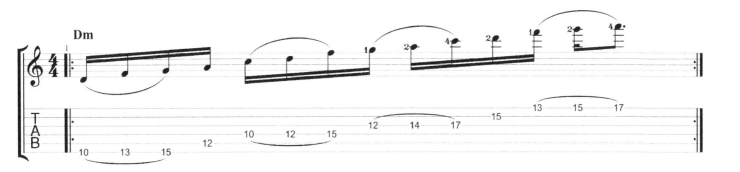

Example 5u:

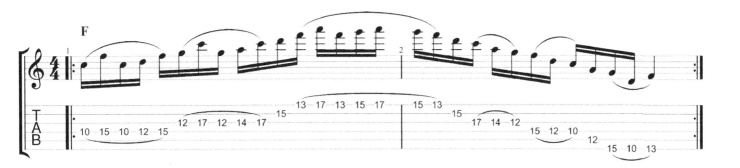

To play Example 5v as written, keep to the sextuplet subdivisions indicated, even when the melodic units switch between fives and sixes on the three-note strings.

Example 5v:

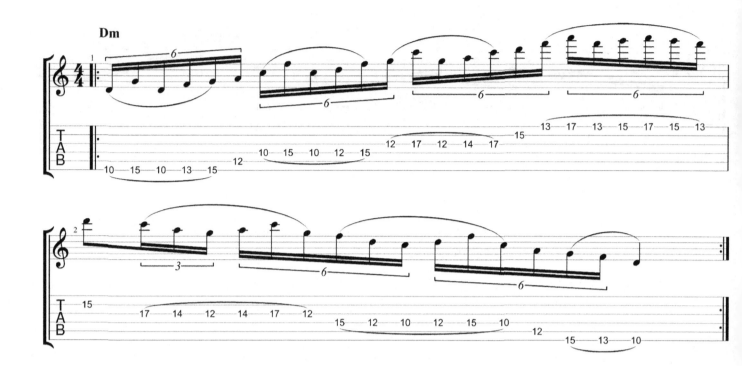

Finally, in pentatonic land, the three-note-per-string format can create some vast fretboard-spanning licks in the style of masters like Brett Garsed.

Example 5w maps out the format using the A Minor pentatonic and Examples 5x to 5z provide sequencing ideas in the Garsed style.

Example 5w:

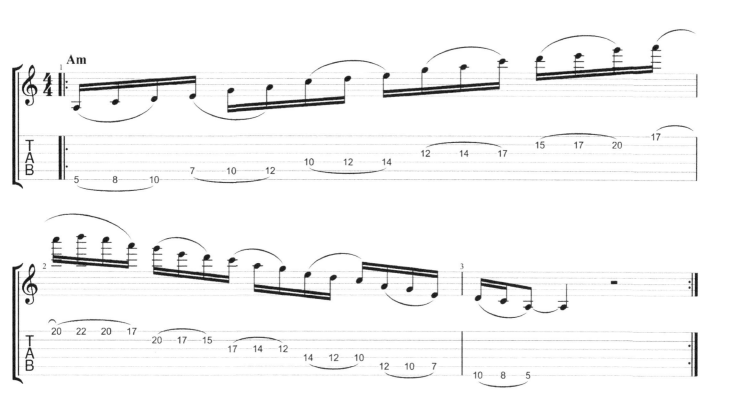

Example 5x:

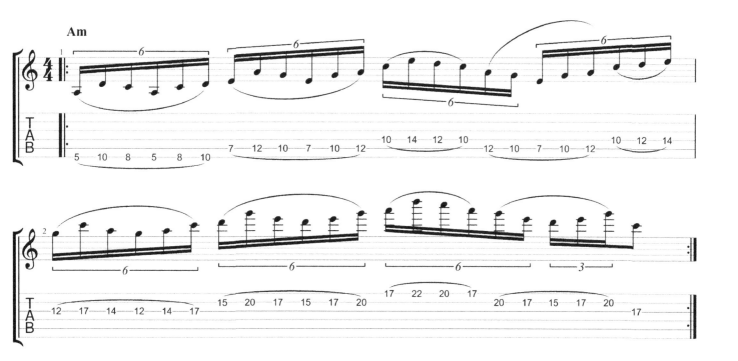

Example 5y:

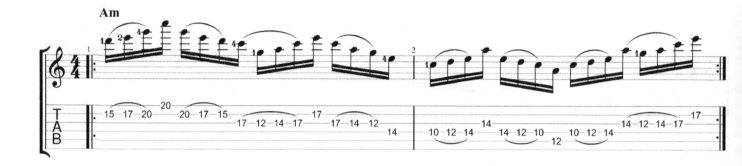

Example 5z:

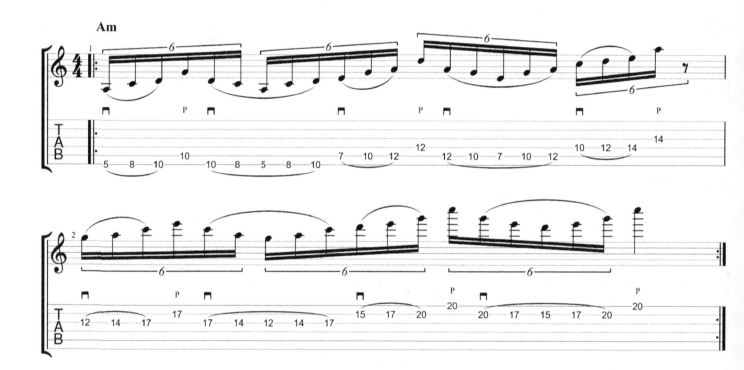

In Chapter Nine, fragments of these pentatonic forms will be combined with diatonic scale patterns.

Chapter Six: Chromatic Passing Tones

Chromatic passing tones are notes that don't belong to the key but are used above and below the diatonic notes. Passing tones from outside the key can create colour, build interest and maximise the number of notes accessible to the fretting hand for legato passages.

This chapter uses chromatic passing tones without forsaking the desired tonality of licks. Scale shapes will be used as a framework for passing tones, with an emphasis on *filling in the blanks* using available fingers not already in use on each string.

By the end of the chapter, you'll be able to engage and disengage passing tones to create an array of new rolling legato lines for your lick bag and have a process to follow to create your own licks and patterns.

The three scale boxes below illustrate:

1. The first pattern of the major scale (used here in the context of a D Dorian tonality).

2. The scale with chromatic passing tones between every whole-note space. Where five notes exist on a string, legato slides will be necessary.

3. A scale shape with only one passing tone per string to maintain a four-note-per-string system.

Box three is an excellent device for getting the passing tone flavour without impacting the fingering of the diatonic notes from box one.

D Dorian in 8th position

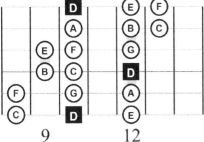 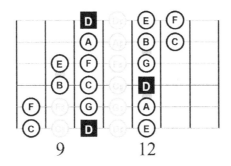 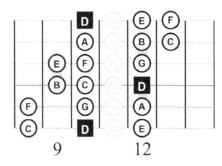

Example 6a is a D Dorian mode played from the 10th fret of the low E string to the 10th fret of the high E string. Take note of the fingers used on each string since the unused fingers will be covering the passing tones in the next example.

Example 6a:

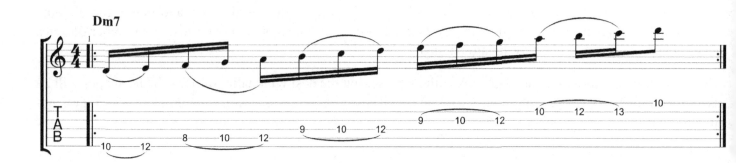

In Example 6b, passing tones are added to the A, D, G and B strings using the third finger of the fretting hand for all except the B string (handled by the second finger).

Example 6b:

Played over a G7 chord and passing through the seventh, sixth and fifth major scale patterns, Example 6c provides a more real-world look at switching between *inside* (diatonic) and *outside* (accidental) notes.

Both the D string and G string feature a small trick to avoiding consecutive semitone overkill. In bar one, beat 3, a row of four notes on the D string is broken up by a note on the G string before returning to the D string for the 10th fret. In bar two, beat one, a similar move occurs between the G string and B string.

In bars three and four, be careful with the timing of position-shifting slides to ensure that the 1/16th notes are played as written.

Example 6c:

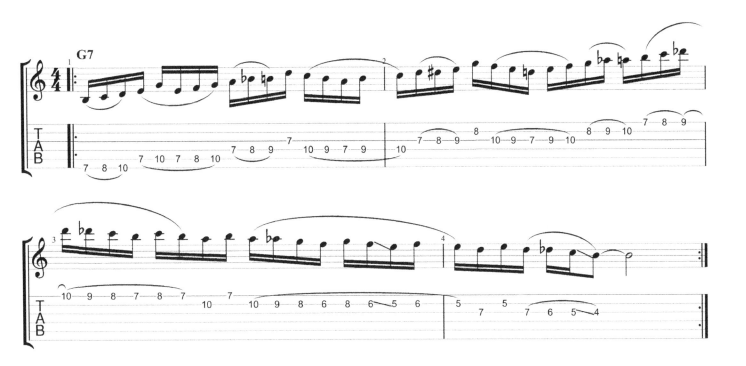

Ideal to be played over an Am triad or Am7 chord, Example 6d dials back the level of chromaticism for a subtle approach with only two passing tones.

Example 6d:

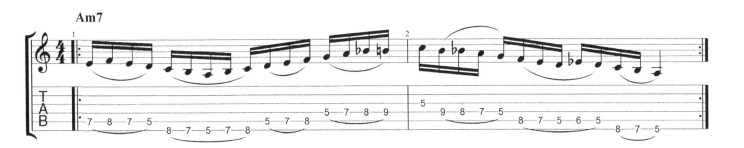

If you have experience playing major scales using the *CAGED System*, you might be familiar with the patterns used as the foundation of Example 6e. Combining the shapes *G* and *A* from CAGED in C Major with selected chromatics, this lick takes another step away from being predictable by mixing sequences and the numbers of notes per string. For best results, memorise and practise this example one bar at a time before getting up to speed.

Example 6e:

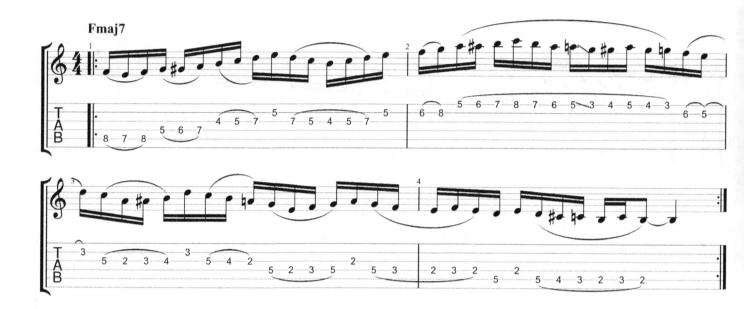

Using passing tones to turn 1-3-1-3-1-3 layouts into 1-4-1-4-1-4, Example 6f works as an Aeolian sounding lick over an Am triad. It can also be transposed a perfect 4th higher over a Dm triad or Dm7 chord.

Example 6f:

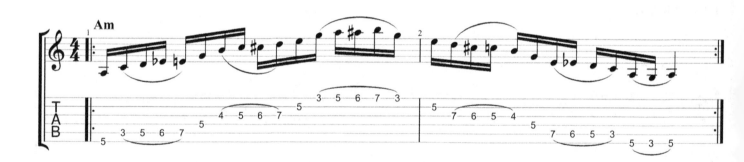

Thanks to one chromatic passing tone per unit, a 3-1-3 unit becomes 3-1-4, creating an eight-note motif. Example 6g features units of eight notes that alternate between beginning on D notes and A notes. To add interest, the lick is displaced by half a beat, thanks to the 1/8th note rest at the start of bar one.

Example 6g:

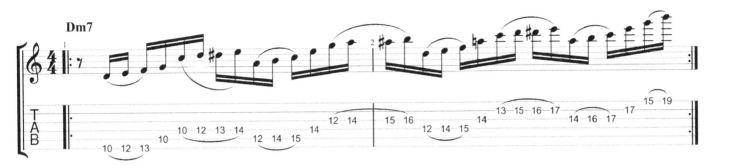

Pentatonic scales make great enclosures for passing tones, as utilised in the next four examples.

Example 6h is based on the classic minor pentatonic box shape in A Minor but can also be transposed to the other pentatonic scales within the key (D Minor and E Minor).

Example 6h:

With a small chromatic twist at the end of each string pair, Example 6i uses the pentatonic layout of Example 5y. For additional lick mileage, each two-beat portion of this example can be looped multiple times before moving on to the next.

Example 6i:

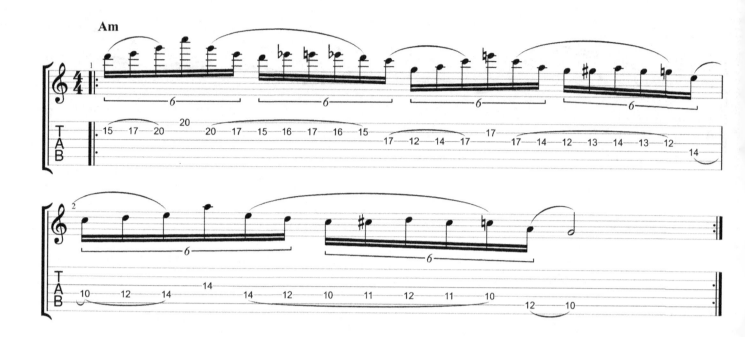

Example 6j begins as a combination of the D Minor pentatonic scale and passing tones, but the inclusion of a D Dorian scale run in bar two makes the combined lick specifically suited to ii chords.

Example 6j:

Played over a C chord, Example 6k displays a very overt use of chromatic passing tones using streams of hammer-ons, pull-offs and slides to get the most mileage out of the high E and G strings. Groupings of septuplets and sextuplets indicate suggested marker points for you to arrive at using the beats of each bar.

Example 6k:

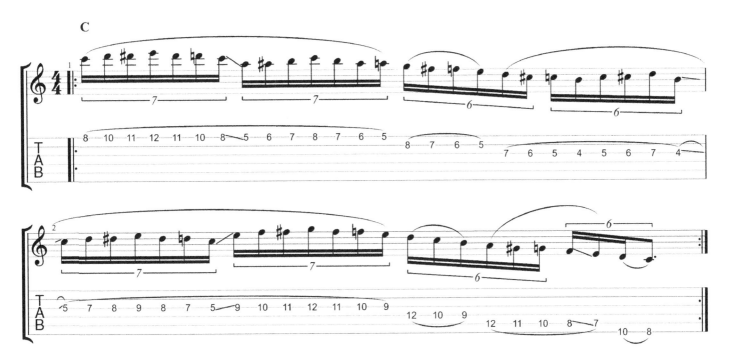

Bonus Tips for Chromatic Passing Tones

While the bulk of this book is about techniques and their many applications, some additional suggestions might help you get the most out of the flavour of chromaticism.

Tension is best accompanied by *release*

When it comes to tonality, the notes we play are either *inside* (belonging to the scale at hand) or *outside* (everything else). The power of passing tones is not just in the tension they create, but in the release when passing tones are resolved to something pleasant, like a chord tone. The longer you spend playing outside the key, the more pressure there is on delivering a resolution.

In the *filling in the blanks* approach used in this chapter, it should be easy to remember where the *in* notes are. Make sure that you don't get so carried away with passing tones that you lose sight of where the safe notes are.

Too much of a good thing

Passing tones are often taught from the perspective of *spicing up your playing*. Keeping with the culinary comparison, you wouldn't cook a steak with twice its weight in pepper. Likewise, chromaticism – at least in the development stage – shouldn't overpower a scale to the point where its tonality is lost in a sink full of semitones. Try to apply passing tones in a measured, tasteful manner.

Ratio Concepts

A methodical way to start applying your passing tone ideas is what I call *ratio concepts*. An inside/outside ratio allocates certain bars or beats to chromatic exploration, using the rest of the time to establish tonality by playing in the key.

For three bars of a four-bar cycle, you could commit to playing in key, and use the fourth bar to go completely experimental with passing tones, resolving in the next repeat of bar one. You might come up with other ratios, like two bars inside, two bars outside. For a beat-based approach, try assigning beats of bars to passing tones, like the fourth beat of every bar, or the last two beats of every second bar etc.

The concept might seem too formulaic, but is a practical way to keep the use of passing tones in check.

Chapter Seven: Legarpeggios

Triads and arpeggios are normally associated with alternate and sweep picking techniques. Besides outlining the notes of a chord, arpeggios employ wider intervals than scales and shorter distances between the high and low registers of the guitar.

This chapter covers some layouts and sequences to include arpeggios in your legato approach. Since many arpeggios partially or exclusively utilise one-note-per-string layouts, hammer-ons from nowhere will be an important device for execution. Noise control will be a crucial part of playing the licks in this chapter cleanly and accurately.

To begin, Example 7a features an A Minor triad on the first three strings. Hammer-ons from nowhere begin each string. As with other hammer-only licks in this book, a careful balancing act between picking hand muting and fretting hand string control is crucial. Before speeding this drill up, ensure that each note is accurately and evenly fretted with consistent attack.

Example 7a:

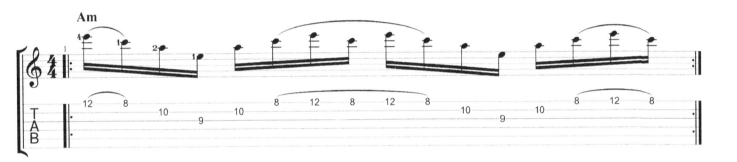

Example 7b applies the sequence from the previous drill to the triads of D Minor, C Major, A Minor and G Major. Your goal in this example is to shift positions without affecting tone or timing, particularly from the C Major triad to the A Minor triad, which both occupy the 12th fret of the high E string in the transition.

Example 7b:

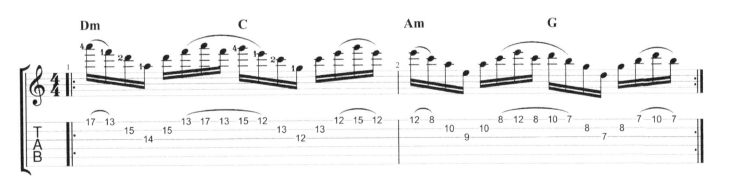

One way to approach larger shapes is to combine the flow of ascending sweep picking with the fretting hand leverage of descending hammers from nowhere. This combo is especially useful when tapping is required.

In Example 7c, a six-string A Minor triad is approached with ascending sweep picking and descending legato.

Example 7c:

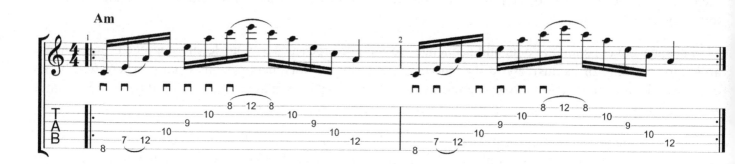

If you've seen Joe Satriani perform the track *The Mystical Potato Head Groove Thing*, you may have noticed a section in which he places his right hand across the strings behind the fretting hand for an arpeggio lick (2:19 on the recorded version). A combination of function and stagecraft, this overhand muting technique allows the picking hand to completely silence the strings while the fretting hand executes an all-hammer arpeggio in both directions.

Example 7d is performed on the audio using the overhand technique. The advantage of this approach is that it is easy to apply and remove and requires no rolling on and off. With the picking hand in the overhand muting position, it's easy to sequence the A Minor triad in this example and focus on hammering the right notes with a consistent dynamic.

Example 7d:

Branching out into extended arpeggios, Example 7e uses the overhand mute while the fretting hand spells out Major Ninth arpeggios over matching chords.

Example 7e:

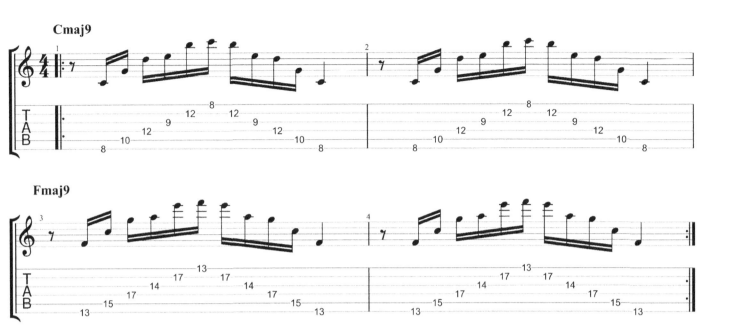

For Example 7f, the picking hand can resume its normal position as the fretting hand uses hammer-ons and sliding position shifts to execute the four triads. Aim to keep your hammer-ons, slides and pull-offs consistent in volume and timing.

Example 7f:

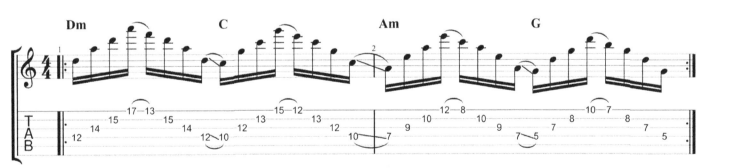

A good exercise for warming up and improving your all-hammer arpeggio chops involves running through every diatonic arpeggio using one zone of the fretboard. With various shapes for seventh arpeggios in the key of C Major, Example 7g maps the root, 3rd, 5th and 7th of each scale degree within a five-fret range.

Example 7g:

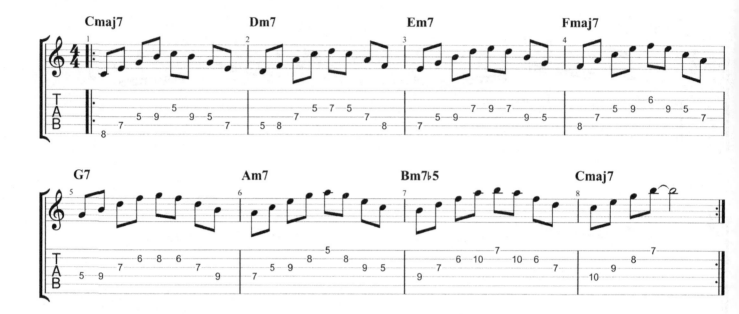

Another helpful approach for seventh arpeggios covers the four notes of the arpeggio in string pairs across three octaves. Played from the lowest fretted position, Example 7h maps out C Major Seventh arpeggios, beginning with the second inversion before moving to the third inversion, root position and first inversion. Example 7i repeats the process for the A Minor Seventh arpeggio, beginning with the third inversion.

Example 7h:

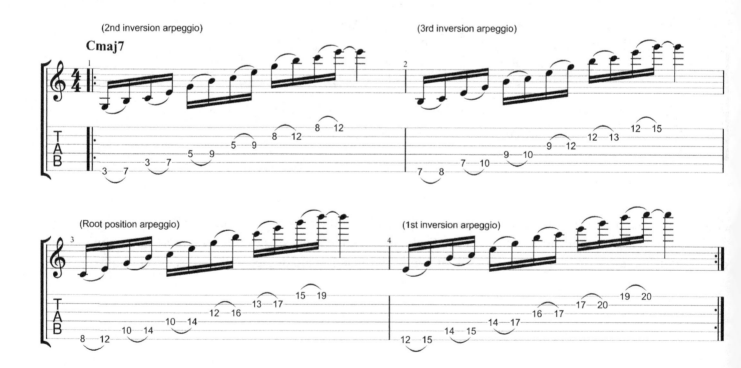

Example 7i:

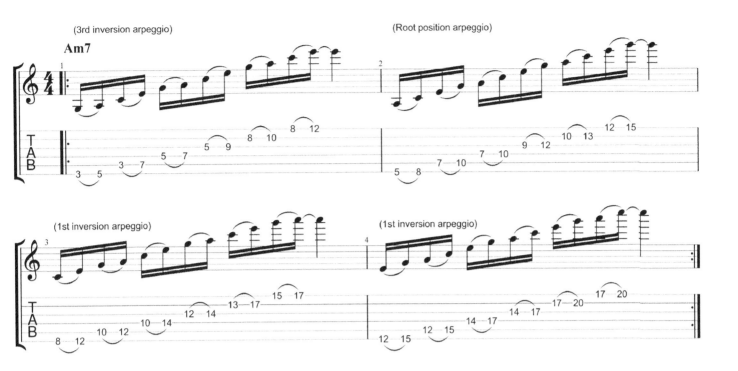

Applying sequences to 2NPS seventh arpeggios, Examples 7j and 7k take a six-note melodic unit and phrase it in 1/16th notes. Bars one and two of both examples are answered with descending versions in bars three and four. The ascents are articulated with hybrid picking. A finger pluck is used to begin the descents and to articulate each of the single-note strings the rest of the way down.

Example 7j:

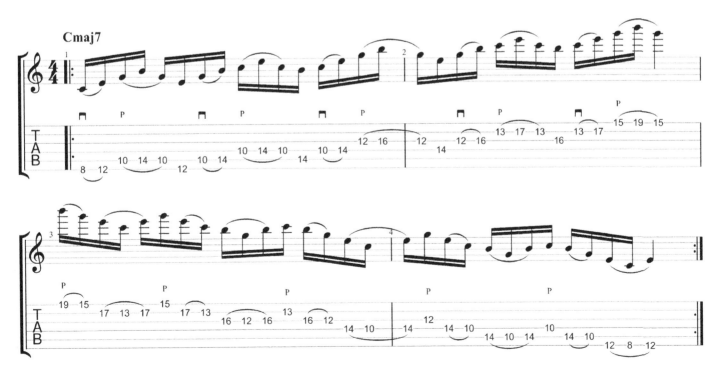

Example 7k:

Example 7l applies ascending and descending fours to a G Dominant Seventh arpeggio (1, 3, 5, b7). A swybrid picking approach works well for the ascending sequence in bars one and two. In the descent, only hammer-ons from nowhere and pull-offs should be required, with one exception. On the 4th beat of bar four, the G note on the 5th fret of the D string requires the picking hand since the index finger is busy rolling out of the previous note.

Example 7l:

Using a mixed number approach, Example 7m alternates between one and three-chord tones per string using major seventh, minor seventh, dominant seventh and minor seventh (flat 5) arpeggios from the key of C Major. In these shapes, sliding position shifts are handled by the index finger in both directions.

Example 7m:

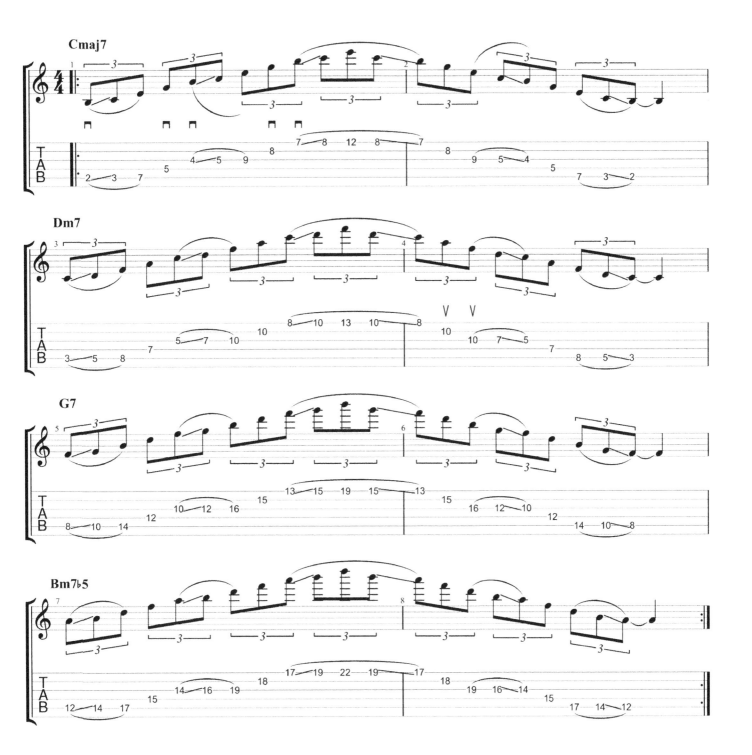

Now that you have a few different arpeggio strategies for legato, it's vital to integrate them with scale-based lines within licks. The last three examples do so with the arpeggio forms of Example 7m.

Example 7n offers a seamless transition between the notes of the C Major scale (F Lydian) and a 3-1-3-1-3 F Major Seventh arpeggio.

Example 7n:

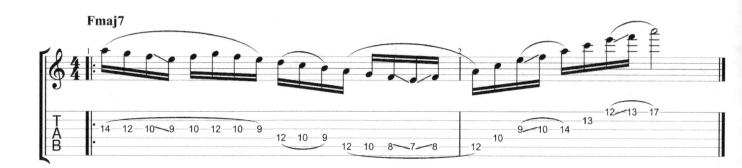

Example 7o uses the framework of a G Dominant Seventh arpeggio to add one extra note (A) to the A string, G string and high E string in bar one while sticking to the arpeggio in bar two.

Example 7o:

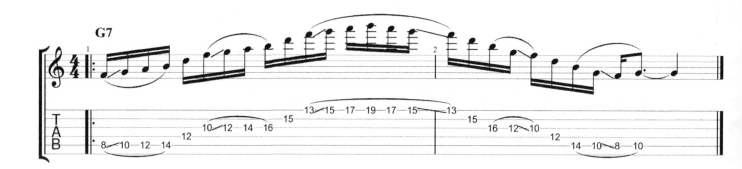

To complete this chapter, Example 7p represents another fully-formed, solo-ready lick suited to an A Aeolian tonality. At the end of the book, lines like this will be combined with many of the other concepts to create *Monster Licks*.

Example 7p:

Chapter Eight: Styling and Ornamentation

Throughout the previous chapters, you've accumulated a wealth of concepts for your legato vocabulary and technique. Taking it a step further, this chapter delves into additional musical and technical devices to inspire your improvisation and allow expressive personalisation to develop within your legato playing.

By the end of this chapter, you will have incorporated the following:

- *Whammy bar technique*: dips and pre-dips, vibrato and horn emulation

- *Rubato:* borrowing and returning time within phrases

- *Burst phrasing*: a staggered time feel made famous by Joe Satriani and Steve Vai.

- *Staccato Legato*: an oxymoron in name, but a useful dynamic device!

If your guitar is fitted with a vintage-style tremolo, make sure it is well set up to enable strings to return to pitch. If your guitar is not equipped with a moving bridge at all, jump ahead to Example 8e.

Whammy Bar Technique

A whammy bar *dip* is a simple but effective way of rearticulating a note that is already ringing. While the note is sustained, a small tap and release of the bar creates a subtle scoop sound in which the note is lowered by an interval like a quarter-tone or semitone before quickly returning to pitch.

In Example 8a, whammy bar dips are used in beats 1-3 of bar one and beats 1 and 2 of bar two. The dips imply a 1/8th note rhythm within the applicable beats.

Example 8a:

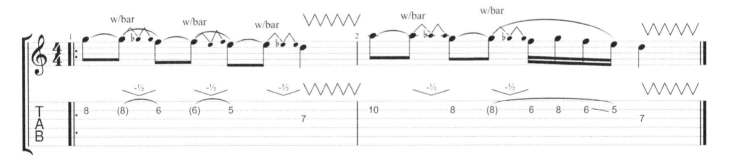

A *pre-dip* is a scoop of the whammy bar that occurs coming into the articulation of a note rather than after it. In the tablature, the marking indicates that pre-dipped notes will start flat and be brought up to pitch.

In bar one of Example 8b, a slide on the B string from the 8th fret to the 10th fret is embellished with a pre-dip on the 10th fret. The same move occurs in bar two from the 7th fret to the 9th fret of the G string. If done correctly, you'll hear the correct pitch of each note in the position shift, with the semitone in between implied with the whammy bar.

Vibrato is also applied using the bar. Whammy vibrato is different from finger vibrato since the bar can move above and below the fretted pitch.

Example 8b:

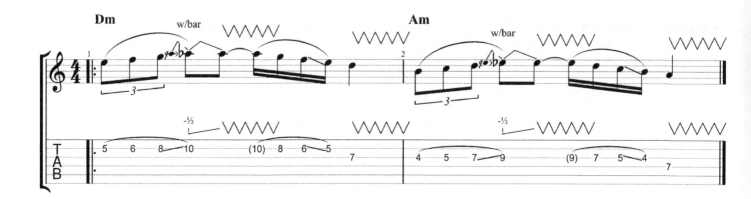

In Example 8c, a pre-dip is placed at the beginning of each beat in bar one. For longer notes like the last note in bar two, experiment with a slower reversal of the pre-dip to emulate a vocal or horn-like approach.

Example 8c:

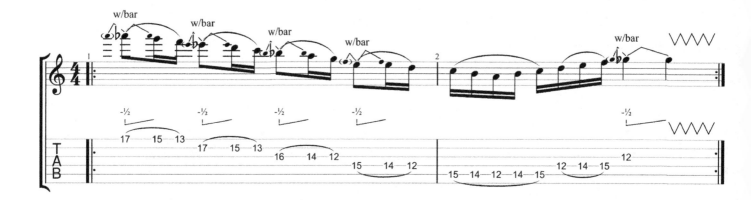

Example 8d is another faux-horn lick that includes the three whammy bar techniques covered so far and introduces a fourth: the *flutter*. In contrast to the small push of a whammy dip, a flutter is an upward pull of the bar that snaps back after release, causing a dramatic *gargle* sound. The flutter in this example occurs on the last note of bar one as it ties over into bar two.

Example 8d:

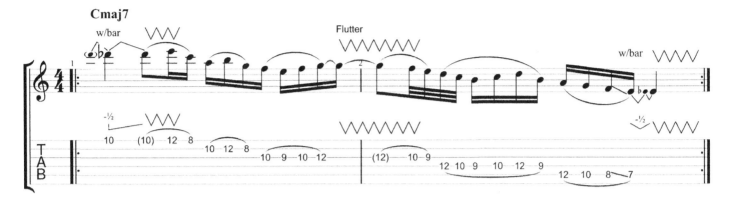

Rubato (Robbed or Borrowed Time)

In Italian *rubato* literally means *robbed*. In phrases that use rubato, expression is achieved by quickening or slackening the time feel without altering the overall tempo. I prefer to use the description *borrowed time* when talking about rubato because what is taken should also be returned. Where some notes are lengthened, others will be shortened.

Demonstrating rubato, the next few phrases compare straightforward notation to the result of borrowing and returning note duration. The audio for these examples will display a true *before and after*.

Example 8e is our first straightforward phrase, played on the audio with strict adherence to the notated rhythm.

Example 8e:

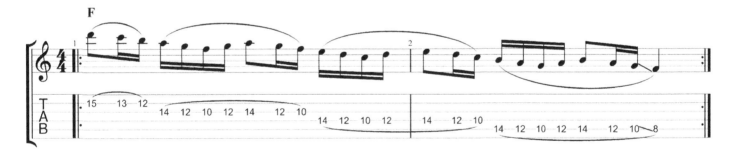

Holding selected notes longer and speeding up others to complete the phrase within the same two bars, Example 8e2 is trickier to sight-read but sounds way more expressive. This is just one way to apply a lot of rubato to a phrase, so after listening to the audio and studying the notation, experiment with your own *push and pull* time feel of the previous example.

Example 8e2:

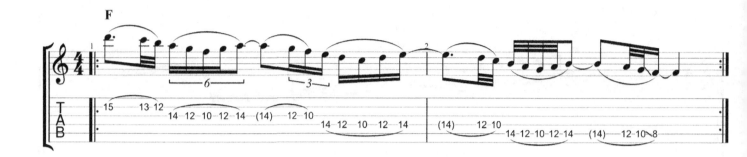

To take a step back and develop a knack for rubato, start with a simple scale shape, then explore your options. In Examples 8f and 8f2, a C Major scale pattern is played firstly as straight 1/16th notes (8f), then deviated with different note groupings (8f), including a nonuplet grouping in bar one, beats 3 and 4.

Example 8f:

Example 8f2:

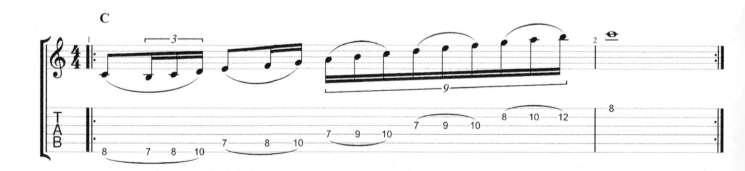

As you develop your command of rubato, maintain your awareness of where beats are, targeting specific marker points to lock back into the beat.

Burst Phrasing (Ornamentation)

Legato works well as a vehicle for *ornamentation*, a way of embellishing a melody. Ornaments are notes that are not crucial to the main melodic line but provide interest, variety and another option for expression, often played as fast notes that circle the important notes of a melody.

Guitarists Joe Satriani and Steve Vai are renowned for ornamented phrasing, aided by small bursts of legato before, after, or around melody notes.

Example 8g begins with three 1/4 note triplets followed by a descending legato phrase.

Example 8g:

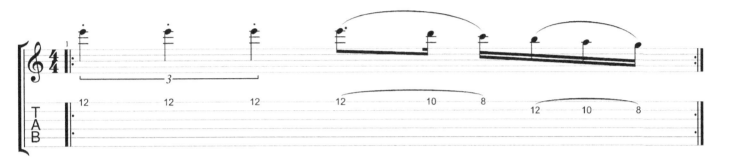

In Example 8h, the four E notes on the 12th fret of the high E string are preceded by C and D notes in quick hammer-on bursts. For extra drama, a rubato effect is created by lengthening the E note on beat 3 and rushing the remaining notes as a sextuplet.

Example 8h:

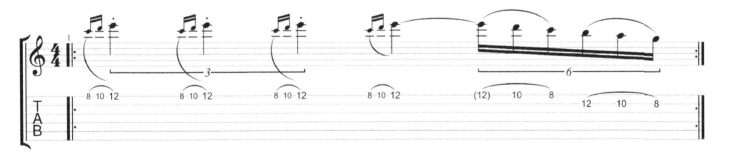

Example 8i, played as a sliding 1/4 note scale fragment would make for a boring lick. Using bursts of 1/32nd notes after each melody note, Example 8j highlights the ascending and descending notes of the previous example but provides a far more exciting alternative.

Example 8i:

Example 8j:

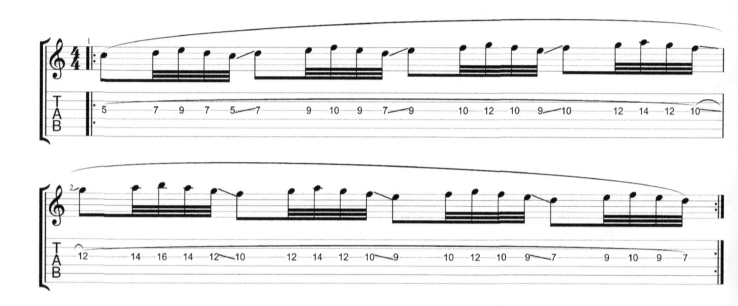

Example 8k contrasts the simple melody of bars one and two with the 1/32nd note ornamentations of bars three and four, executed with legato, hybrid picking and slides. In both halves of the lick, the main melody notes land in the same spots. Bars three and four can also be played as straight 1/16th notes for an extra descending sequence for your lick bag.

Example 8k:

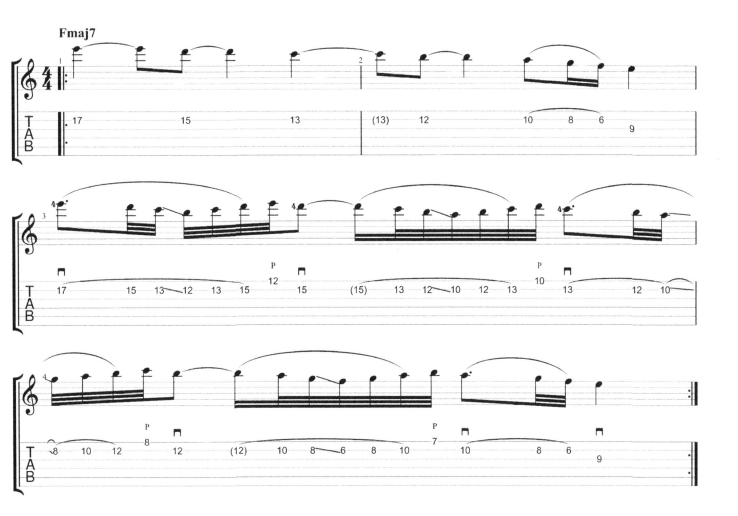

Staccato Legato

Staccato Legato is a phrase I coined in the early 2010s for some YouTube content that explored the technique of muting legato lines to create new options for attack and dynamics. Staccato (meaning *detached* or *separated*) and legato (*tied together*) are musical opposites according to the dictionary, but the combination of fretting hand slurs and picking hand muting creates a sound that is unlike either true legato or picking.

Any legato line can become a muted one, but hammer-ons from nowhere work particularly well in this approach.

Example 8l is a two-string drill played without any pick strokes. With your picking hand in a palm-muting stance, repeat the lick with various amounts of muting pressure to experiment with the *dynamic range*.

Dynamic range is the difference between the softest and loudest notes in a phrase. Very light muting will allow the pitch of the notes to come through and heavy muting will create a very percussive tone with indeterminate pitch.

Example 8l:

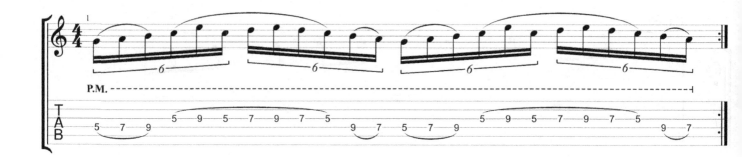

Using the notes from the previous drill, Example 8m alternates between the fluid sound of bar one and the restricted sound of bar two. The amount of pressure applied in the mute will decide how much dynamic range exists between the two bars.

Example 8m:

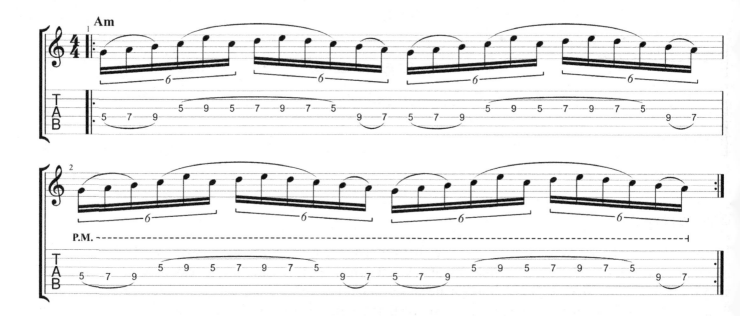

For the muting aspect of this technique, any scale can become a practice drill. In Example 8n, a muted C Major scale ascends from the low E string to the G string, becoming unmuted at the halfway mark and descending back to the low E string. This can be practised in free-time but is notated in two sets of 1/16th note *undecuplets* – a feel similar to sextuplets but with a slight lag since there are twenty-two notes instead of twenty-four.

Example 8n:

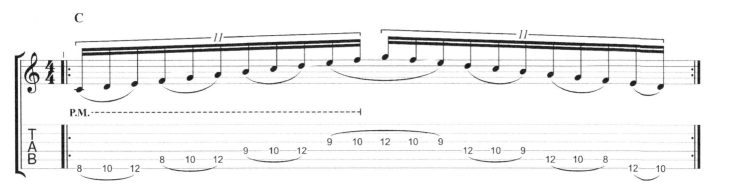

Bringing the pick back into play, Example 8o is a string skipping lick with muted and unmuted portions. The higher string in each two-beat pair should ring nice and clear and be contrasted by heavy muting on each lower string.

Example 8o:

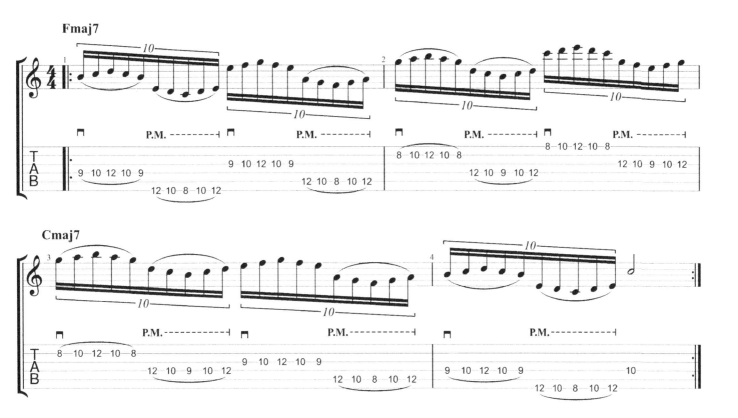

On my debut album *The Master Plan* (2002), the opening track, called *Kryptica*, featured a lick that I'm still often asked about. Using a sound that I describe as *cascading overtones*, the fretting-hand figure in Example 8p repeats while the palm mute (beginning on bar one, beat 3) slides inward from the bridge to the neck pickup.

The sliding mute passes through different harmonics to create an attention-grabbing sound that almost sounds like an effects pedal. To get the right overtones, be sure not to mute too heavily.

Example 8p:

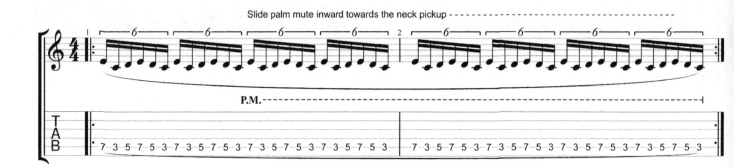

Chapter Nine: Monster Licks

This is where it all comes together! Using all of the techniques and musical devices covered in previous chapters, this collection of licks will put your dexterity, timing and finger tone to the test.

The audio for this chapter includes backing tracks at full speed and half speed. To practise in other increments, computer programs like *Audacity*, *Transcribe* and *Riffstation* will allow you to find the tempo best-suited to your ability as you progress.

Straight out of the gate, Example 9a fuses the D Dorian mode with chromatic passing tones, pentatonics, string skipping and muted legato! A *push and pull* rhythmic feel is created by regularly switching between 1/16th notes and 1/16th note triplets and sextuplets.

Example 9a:

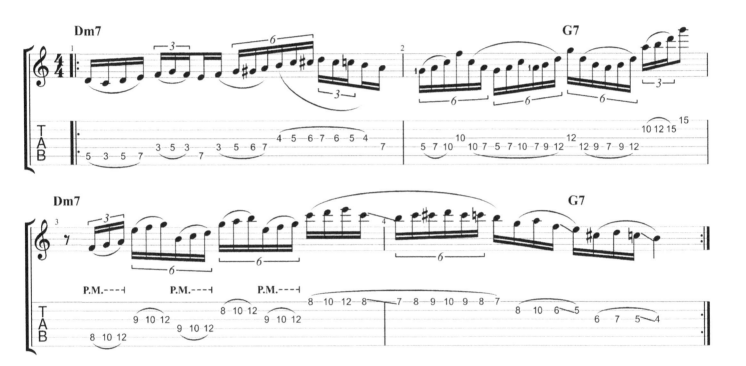

In Example 9b, the 1/16th note phrasing of bars one, two and four are contrasted with rhythmic bursts on the G string. The ascending lick in bar four is created from a two-note-per-string F Major Seventh arpeggio.

Example 9b:

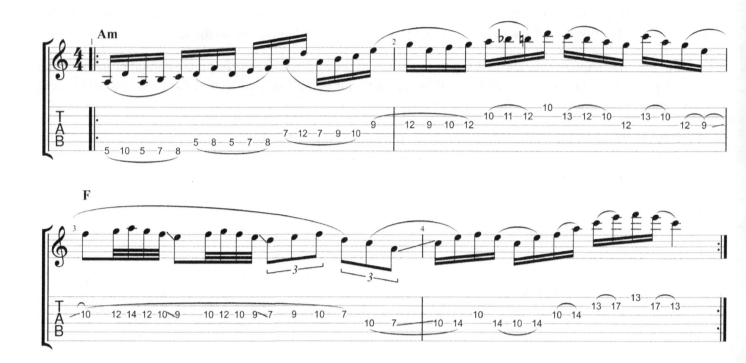

Played over alternating C Major Seventh and F Major Seventh chords, Example 9c includes 1-3-1-3-1-3 scale layouts (bars one and two), scales sequences with additional passing tones (bars three and four), a three-octave shifting pattern (bars five and six), and C Major Seventh arpeggios (bar seven) before concluding with the descending run of bar eight.

Over an F Major Seventh chord, the notes of the C Major Seventh arpeggio represent the perfect 5th, major 7th, major 9th and augmented 4th (11th) of the F Lydian mode.

Example 9c:

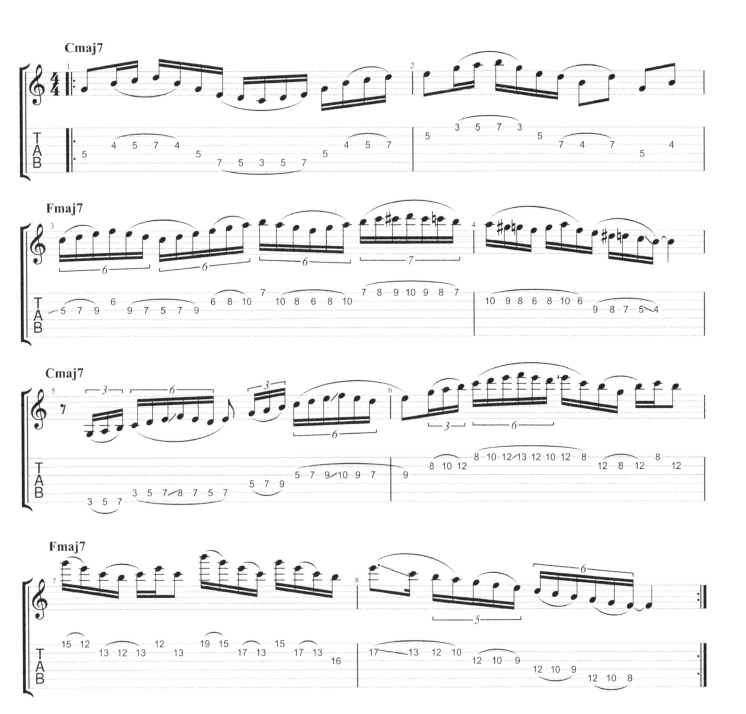

Example 9d is played exclusively over a G Dominant Seventh chord to produce the Mixolydian tonality throughout. Of particular melodic interest are the arpeggios in bar two (crossing over into bar three) which use B Minor Seventh (flat 5, flat 9), G Dominant Ninth and F Major Ninth arpeggios as a way of cutting through the scale in wider intervals.

The string-skipping in bars seven and eight gets wider with each instance, so be sure to maintain the timing notated. The low E string is muted every time while each higher string is unmuted and accelerated to 1/32nd note bursts.

Example 9d:

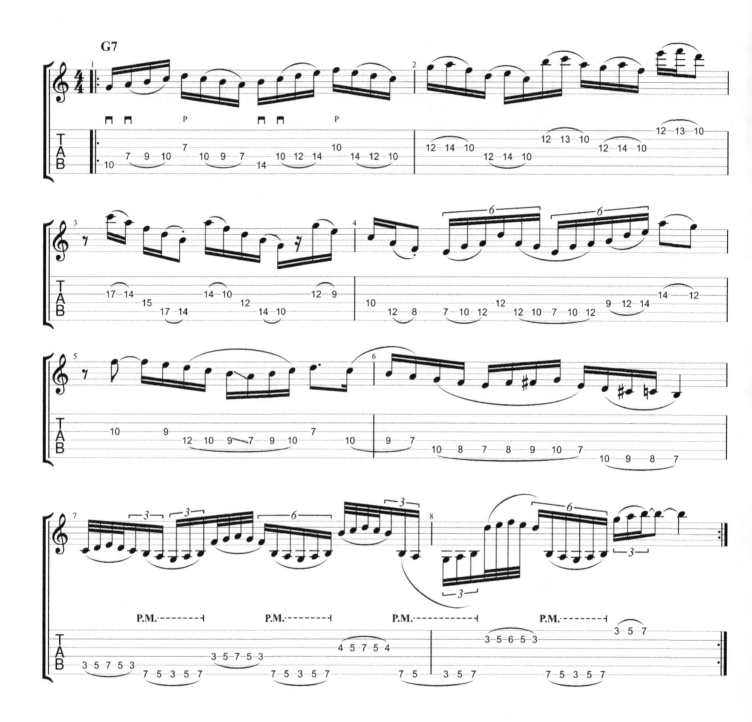

Applying some of the whammy bar techniques covered, the next study begins slow and allows time for dips, pre-dips, a flutter and a small dive bomb. Other notable attributes include E Minor Seventh arpeggios in bar three, single-string burst phrasing in bar four, and a 4-1-4-1-4 scale layout in bar six.

Example 9e:

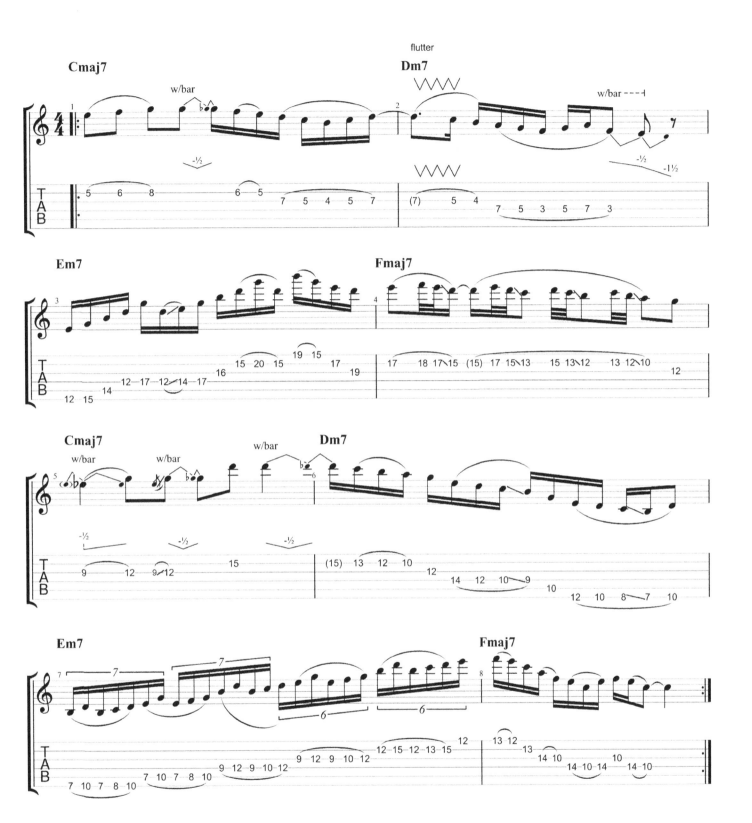

To finish the chapter (and the book!), Example 9f is played over a I – IV – V progression in A Minor. The V chord in bars seven and eight is a dominant seventh chord formed from the 5th degree of A Harmonic Minor.

Melodically, bars one and two combine a 1-3 Aeolian pattern, a six-string A Minor arpeggio and a 2NPS C Major Seventh arpeggio. Continuing over the same A Minor Seventh chord, bar three sequences a 3NPS scale pattern while bar four descends along the G string using whammy bar dips.

In bars five and six, look out for the alternating four-note and three-note-per-string patterns, the former of which is fretted using all four fingers rather than slides.

Borrowing from A Harmonic Minor, bars seven and eight play host to a G# Diminished Seventh arpeggio played in descending fours. The relationship between diminished arpeggios and the harmonic minor scale is covered in my book, *Neoclassical Speed Strategies for Guitar*.

Example 9f:

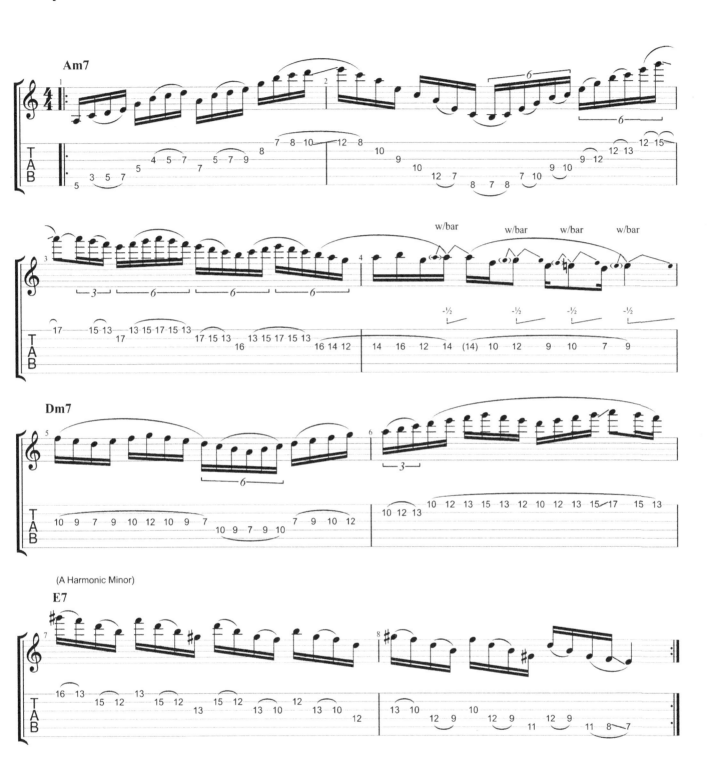

Conclusion

The cool thing about legato as both a musical device and a *guitar-centric* skill set is that it can be used as often or as seldom as your creativity calls upon it. Whether you build an entire style out of it or use it to contrast the aggression of your picked lines, the material in this book should be applied to real-life playing situations as soon as possible.

Learn the material as-is, but don't just stop there. Adapt the licks, transpose them, reverse them, combine them and see where the journey takes your playing. Similarly, with the mechanical approaches, try all of the options presented and systemise the strongest ideas into a personal blend that represents *your* choices.

I hope this book has been a source of enlightenment for developing a technical command of legato, and that it continues to be a source of inspiration with repeated reading.

Thanks for letting me be your guide to *Legato Guitar Technique Mastery*.

Chris Brooks

More From Chris Brooks

Neo-Classical Speed Strategies for Guitar

Sweep Picking Speed Strategies for Guitar

Advanced Arpeggio Soloing for Guitar

Sweep Picking Speed Strategies for 7-String Guitar

Find out more by scanning the QR code below:

Made in the USA
Middletown, DE
31 January 2021